LEADING

Those You

LOVE

Matthew Miklasz

Copyright © 2024 Matthew Miklasz

All rights reserved.

No part of this book may be reproduced, stored in a retrieval system, or transmitted by any means, electronic, mechanical, photocopying, recording, or otherwise, without written permission from the author.

ISBN (Paperback): 979-8-9919700-7-5
ISBN (eBook): 979-8-9919700-6-8

THE HOLY BIBLE, NEW INTERNATIONAL VERSION®, NIV® Copyright © 1973, 1978, 1984, 2011 by Biblica, Inc.® Used by permission. All rights reserved worldwide.

Scripture quotations are taken from the *Holy Bible,* New Living Translation, copyright © 1996, 2004, 2015 by Tyndale House Foundation. Used by permission of Tyndale House Publishers, Inc., Carol Stream, Illinois 60188. All rights reserved.

The ESV® Bible (The Holy Bible, English Standard Version®). ESV® Text Edition: 2016. Copyright © 2001 by Crossway, a publishing ministry of Good News Publishers. The ESV® text has been reproduced in cooperation with and by permission of Good News Publishers. Unauthorized reproduction of this publication is prohibited. All rights reserved.

New American Standard Bible (NASB) Copyright © 1960, 1962, 1963, 1968, 1971, 1972, 1973, 1975, 1977, 1995 by The Lockman Foundation

Scripture taken from *The Message*. Copyright © 1993, 1994, 1995, 1996, 2000, 2001, 2002. Used by permission of NavPress Publishing Group

Matthew (Matt) has served in the local Church ministry for over thirty years. He was ordained in the Evangelical Free Church of America in 2003. He has authored three books A *Normal Guy, Joy for the Journey,* and *Living with Passion.* He is a coach to several pastors and has been featured on multiple TV shows including Cornerstone TV and Babbie's House and radio. He is a speaker at retreats, conferences, and seminars. He is the Senior Pastor at Faith Evangelical Free Church in Stanley, Wisconsin. He enjoys coaching sports, reading, and helping his beautiful bride Cyndy on their hobby farm. Matt has been married to Cyndy for thirty-three years and is the father to four grown children.

Contact: pastormatt@faithfreestanley.org

Table of Contents

Acknowledgements ix

Testimonials xi

Forward xv

Introduction xvii

Chapter One – The Call to Lead 1

Chapter Two – Leading Yourself 9

Chapter Three – Leading Your Spouse 20

Chapter Four – Leading Your Children 31

Chapter Five – Leading Your Teams 50

Chapter Six – Leading Through Trials 60

Chapter Seven – Leading Through the Fog 68

Chapter Eight – Leading to the End – The Endurance of a Leader 75

Conclusion 81

Appendix 83

Endnotes 85

To Jesus Christ
May this book bring you praise

Acknowledgements

My Bride – I love you and praise God for you. You have time and time again encouraged me in my leadership.

Angela, Benjamin, David, and Emily – I don't know how I was blessed with four. You are loved more than you know and you make this daddy proud.

Dad and Mom – Their love knew no limits and their lessons I still learn from it.

Deb, Linda, Tom, Beth, and Mary – I love that God brought our weird family together. You each make life fun.

Chad and Emily Eichstadt – I value your friendship, your kindness in helping edit this book and your encouragement in sharing the message.

John and Becky Milliren – You two are a gift to me and my family. Thank you for the treasure of your friendship which helps me endure.

Mick Shilts and Bob Rohland – These men came to my mind several times in writing this book. Although God has called these two men home their impact on my life and leadership continues.

Faith EFC Family – I am humbled and privileged to serve you. I love you all.

Testimonials

I have known Pastor Matt for over twenty-five years! When I say he is the real deal, he really is! I have seen him in different ministry roles and also serve the body of Christ as a shepherd, Pastor, teacher, and alongsider! Wherever Pastor Matt has served, the people around him have been blessed. The main thing for Pastor Matt is he always points people to Jesus!!

This book is the heart and soul of a man that I have seen persevere in ministry and life.

Matt shares truths from God's word and his personal experiences as a follower of Jesus devoted to listening to God's leading in His life!
Rob Weise
Director of Community and Events – Forest Lakes District of EFCA

Nothing lends credibility to an author quite like life. We have journeyed through life with Matt as our friend (and Pastor) for over thirty years. Self-proclaimed "normal guy" Matt has shown how to walk the talk. Honest and authentic, Matt is genuine, cares deeply, and is a source of encouragement when life takes painful turns. He is a faithful friend who will lead you to the truth found in God's extraordinary love.
John and Becky Milliren
Close friends and educators

Pastor Matt has been my coach, my pastor, & lifelong friend. When I think of him as a leader, this verse from 1 Thessalonians 2:8 comes to mind: "So having great love toward you, we were willing to impart to you not only the Gospel of God but also our own lives, because you were dear to us." Pastor Matt has great love for those he leads, I would say a tenacious kind of love, that makes them feel incredibly valued like they are his very best friend. He puts his whole heart into relationships. He puts all the chips on the table. This book is not just wise words, but a life poured out for the sake of Christ and his Body. Reading this book is an invitation from the Lord to lead with your whole heart and discover His! Be blessed as you read this very necessary book!
Joy VanDeLoo
Missionary with Cru

What sets Matt apart is his genuine passion for helping others. His experiences and reflections instill a sense of trust and encouragement, making you feel supported on your journey. The way he articulates complex spiritual concepts into actionable steps is nothing short of remarkable. I had the profound pleasure of reading Matt Miklasz's latest work, *Leading Those You Love*, and I can confidently say that his insights are both practical and transformative. Matt's unique ability to weave together practical knowledge and deep wisdom makes this book a must-read for anyone seeking to live a Christ-centered life. From the very first chapter, Matt invites readers to explore the core principles that shape a life grounded in faith. His approach is refreshingly relatable, offering real-world applications that resonate with everyday challenges.

Chad Eichstadt
High School teacher and coach at Owen Withee High School in Wisconsin.

We have known Matt for over thirty years. He has not only led us, but he has led our children and also now our grandchildren. Matt is a man who loves the Lord and clearly has been called to pastor. Over the years, he has never shied away from addressing the hard issues that Christians face every day by leading them to the scriptures. He is a leader who serves as an example of walking in truth and is an encourager. We can say without a doubt that his newest book *Leading Those You Love* is a must-read and will lead you and others to become God's hands and feet in the places you lead. He will share his love for Christ with everyone who comes in contact with him, whether meeting him in person or in the pages of his books."

Jerry and Lori Czubakowski
Jerry is an elder at Faith EFC Church in Stanley, WI.
Lori is a former Administrative Assistant at Faith EFC.

I don't ever remember a time in my life that I didn't know Matt. I have known him as my big brother's friend, my coach, my youth pastor, my senior pastor, and now my coworker. Matt has always had the gift to speak truth into a person and help them see they are capable of more than they believe and come across leaving you feeling loved and seen. This book does both. Matt speaks Biblical truth on the many ways you can and even need to step up as a leader whether it be in the home or other areas of your life. It also provides real-life examples filled with truth and love to go along with it. Not only does he talk the talk, but he also walks the walks. This book will leave you feeling ready to lead with love in your own life.

Jaime Barth
Children's Ministry Coordinator
Faith EFC Stanley, WI.

I have known Matt for over thirty years. Over these years, not only has Matt led me, but I have witnessed him leading others. Matt truly is an exceptional leader with immense wisdom and experience leading within his home, the church, and the community. We are all leaders in some way, and you will discover multiple truths about leading those you love from this book. It gives biblical insight and practical applications of leadership that will inspire you to become a better and more intentional leader.

Sarah Alger
Administrative Assistant at Faith EFC

During my time as an associate under Matt, I saw the powerful impact of his leadership philosophy – placing people before tasks. He consistently demonstrated that leading with love means caring for the whole person, not just focusing on their role or performance. I always felt valued and supported, not merely as an employee but as a person. That's what makes his approach to *Leading Those You Love* so transformative. He offers a heart-centered guide for leaders who want to inspire, uplift, and truly invest in those they serve.

Matt Peters
Associate Pastor
Valleybrook Church – Eau Claire, WI.

Forward

Leading Those You Love

Leadership is desperately needed in our world today. Proverbs 11:14 *"Where there is no guidance* (leadership) *a people falls..."*

Leadership at its core is influence, throughout my life, I have interacted with individuals who have told me they are leaders, and my response is "If you are a leader, who is following you?"

Matthew Miklasz's loving leadership and influence inspire people. Matt is the kind of leader that those who know him want to follow. We see too many leaders who seem to lead for their own interest or benefit.

In *Leading Those You Love,* Matt identifies the different spheres of leadership in one's life and then he outlines avenues toward authentic servant leadership. This book is for all who aspire to have a deep influence on lives.

In every leader connection it is important to remember the encouragement from scripture for love to permeate every encounter. 1 Corinthians 16:14 *"Let all that you do be done in love."*

Jon Payne
Forest Lakes EFCA District Superintendent

Introduction

I have been in leadership roles and positions for forty years and have learned far more than any book could convey. As I reflect on my experience as a leader in the home, marketplace, and the church I have developed deep convictions. I lay in my bed one night not long ago considering revising an earlier book I had written to include thoughts and lessons I wanted to include. As I considered what that would look like, I sensed God impressing upon me to write a new one. That night, I experienced what could be described as great clarity of direction. The clarity and content of the message of this book have come with assurance to my mind and spirit. The message being: Leading those you love so as to have a deep and lasting influence in their lives.

As a fellow leader, I know firsthand that leadership can be complex and takes wisdom, courage, and strength. Even more, it needs love and grace. I appreciate the unique challenges leaders face whether in marriage, parenting, or in the workplace and Church for I have led and am leading in all these contexts.

I want to come alongside you and bring encouragement. I find the words in this book especially relevant for all of you who:

- Want to leave a deep and lasting impact on your wife, child, coworkers, and congregations.
- Want to renew your passion that can get dampened by the day-to-day demands.
- Want practical ways that lead to deep influence in the various contexts you lead.
- Want to move past the confusion and challenges to a renewed direction.

I want to speak to your hearts as one who has been there in many cases. I have prayed hard over this book trusting God to use my words to encourage you so you may lead those you love into richer experiences in their life. That is to bring a deep influence calling to the deep within others. That is at the heart of what this book is about. I believe God would have me share truths, lessons, and encouragement for anyone who leads in any way. I believe all the qualities that are often referenced regarding leading our homes, churches, and the workplace result in shallow connection and little impact.

In some capacity, everyone will lead someone, and they will lead those somewhere. It bears repeating everyone leads in some way. I believe we all can look at the needs around us and our roles and get overwhelmed and disillusioned even to the point of neglecting or ignoring what we are called to do. Many take steps to lead in their home, marriage, or the workplace only to realize there is something missing. Their position and the work that it entails becomes hard, draining, and at times confusing. When we are overcome, purpose and passion are buried under the weight of expectations, failures, and planning. Our hearts shrink and our impact is limited. Too much attention is given to leadership position and authority and too little on the heart and mind from which true leadership comes. All the well-planned objectives and leadership techniques cannot replace the absence of an expanding heart of grace and the influence that emanates from that inner life.

This book is about influencing others on a deep level. The leaders with deep and lasting influence beyond their life here on earth have this in common: they have a heart that has been and is being cultivated by God and His grace. Their lives are oriented around His work in their hearts and His work through them. It is this inner life marked by grace that connects with others which is the avenue to a deep and lasting influence. Proverbs 4:23 says,

> Guard your heart above all else,
> for it determines the course of your life. (NLT)

There is a missing ingredient in leadership within the various contexts of leadership. It is the heart. A heart that loves. A heart that is vulnerable. A heart being changed by the grace of God and made alive to express that grace.

It is becoming increasingly evident the one thing lacking in leadership in homes, churches, and organizations is grace. If that seems simplistic in stating, you are right. If you believe love and grace are simple in living out in leadership contexts you couldn't be more wrong. Knowing what love looks like in both day-to-day and long-term leadership is not so clear. Through the seasons of leading our marriages, families, coworkers, and teams we find expressions of grace look different and bear fruit in various ways.

I believe there is a vacuum in leadership resources in regard to authenticity in leading and the deep influence that is possible in leadership. I believe God has given me a voice to speak in a way that is honest, relatable, and encouraging. I have read many leadership books, and while containing some really good stuff I too often finished the last page feeling like a loser. Comparisons and calculations left me wondering what I was even doing. Attending conferences at times left me feeling the same way. Gifted speakers and high achievers shared their successes. Leaders of large churches spoke and those of us who lead small churches felt like the little people in the room. Insecurities and failures most certainly contribute to those feelings but there was something else missing. It was like the caramel was missing from the inside of a Milky Way bar. When the caramel is gone, the chocolate on the outside loses its taste.

Leading those you love requires something at the core or it will lose influence. At the core must be something that is lasting. Principles, structures, plans, production reports, profit margins, and a whole host of activities fill up our schedules but lack the deep and lasting influence we long to make. Many of the books and conferences I've been exposed to presented good content. I gleaned helpful principles, beneficial structures, and fruitful practices. Yet something that belonged on the inside was missing.

Many have leadership skills which of course are needed, yet prove limited in their scope of influence without the heart of a leader calling out to others.

Yet this book is not a depressing critique of leadership. It is a clarion call to husbands, dads, coaches, supervisors, church leaders, CEO's and all other contexts of leadership. This call is to get to the heart of what really matters in all those contexts we lead in. It is a call to raise the bar in how we lead.

As a follower of Jesus Christ, I can testify that the good news of the love and grace of Christ frees me from the burden of seeking to minimize or deny reality. We can approach our leadership honestly.

Instead of seeking to simply apply principles, we find love and grace take us where we want to lead. For it is love and grace that brings deep and lasting influence. It is the deep work of grace that leads to this deep influence.

I open my Bible, and I get my concordance, and I look up all occurrences of grace in the Bible. There are 131 uses of grace in the ESV translations—124 in the New Testament. In the New Testament, we see grace emerge primarily in two ways.

Grace as Undeserved Favor

On the one hand, grace is called—and I think it's an absolutely wonderful phrase—"undeserved favor."

> Romans 3:24: "[We] are justified by his grace as a gift, through the redemption that is in Christ Jesus." Grace is what inclines God to give gifts that are free and undeserved by sinners. (ESV)

> Romans 5:15: "If many died through one man's trespass, much more have the grace of God and the free gift by the grace of that one-man Jesus Christ abounded for many." (ESV)

> So, grace is that quality in God that produces free gifts for guilty sinners in salvation. (ESV)

> Romans 11:5–6: So too at the present time there is a remnant, chosen by grace. But if it is by grace, it is no longer on the basis of works; otherwise, grace would no longer be grace. (ESV)

God is indeed the God of grace. He grants His grace freely and abundantly. Our eternal lives depend on it. None of us would be saved if grace were not undeserved favor and were not a quality in the mind of God, in the heart of God, in the nature of God. Ephesians 2:8-9 affirms this,

> For it is by grace you have been saved, through faith—and this is not from yourselves, it is the gift of God—not by works, so that no one can boast. (NIV)

Grace is also used in another sense.

Grace as Power for Living

> 2 Corinthians 9:8: "God is able to make all grace abound to you, so that having all sufficiency in all things at all times, you may abound in every good work." (ESV)

Now, that seems to picture grace as a power or an influence for obedience.

> 2 Corinthians 12:9: Jesus says to Paul, "My grace is sufficient for you, for my power is made perfect in weakness." (ESV)

1 Corinthians 15:10: "By the grace of God I am what I am, and his grace toward me was not in vain. On the contrary, I worked harder [that was the effect of grace] than any of them, though it was not I, but the grace of God that is with me." (ESV)

In all three of those texts—and they're not the only ones—grace is not only a disposition or a quality or an inclination but is an influence or a force or a power or acting of God that works in us to change our capacities for work, obedience and impacting others. This is the discovery we as leaders need to make and embrace. Grace changes and increases our capacity to impact others!

There is a grace that grants us first the power to receive love and the power to give it. There is a grace that changes us, shapes us, and can change and shape our leadership. God's grace brings power into our lives which changes and enlarges our hearts and enlarges our capacity to extend it toward others. Your leadership can bring a deep and lasting influence when fueled by grace. Great leadership begins within. Before any talk of a deep and lasting influence, I must point you to the life-changing and empowering grace of God.

It is my heartfelt prayer that God's work in and through my life, my experiences and the lessons God has taught me will energize, instruct, and set you on a course of leading those you love in transformative ways. I need to state at the outset I believe the Bible is the Word of God and is the lens through which I look at the world, my life, and the topic of leadership. There is no more reliable authority for us to seek that speaks to our lives. When we align our leadership with the Bible, God's Word, and submit to His work in our hearts the places we live and contexts we lead become different. The influence is deeper and lasting. We will see fruitful efforts in the immediate and generational blessing in the long term.

The fact you picked this book up tells me you want more from your context of leading. I am trusting these pages to be a help to you and to give you hope. I remind myself often I only have one shot at this life here on earth and so I want to maximize my time and my impact. I invite you to join me on this journey and trust this book will lead you to places where you can draw from the work of grace inside your heart.

CHAPTER ONE

The Call to Lead

In my mid-twenties, I took inventory of my life in an attempt to discern what I wanted to do vocationally. I recognized through my times of evaluation and reflection that from a young age I found myself in leadership roles. From leading neighborhood kids in organizing games and activities in my grade school years to taking the lead on the teams I played on in High school. I naturally gravitated to taking on the role of captain and leader. When I began working at a wood manufacturing plant in my mid-twenties it wasn't long before I was moved into a supervisor role and then into a larger role which included some management. I also began to work as a volunteer with the youth at the church I attended. After a couple of years, I was asked to take the lead in the youth ministry as a volunteer. The church a year or so later asked me to step on staff as the youth pastor and then elder board and a few years after into the senior pastor role. I also have served as leader of multiple community clergy groups and with some district initiatives. I did not actively pursue or plan a career path toward filling any of these positions. Instead, I felt a strong sense of call. A call rooted in the realization God has designed me and given me a passion to equip, teach, and see people set free to live out their calling. I have said to my wife before, "you could never talk me out of being a pastor. It would be like ripping my heart out". I am that convinced of God's call on my life. So how does one discern that call and how does one steward that call faithfully and fruitfully?

It requires the right posture. To be clear, these postures do not come naturally, and a part of me and you will fight against these. Your biggest threat to leading from these postures will be you. The sin that resides within each of us will pull us toward self and control. Our hearts can be deceptive, and we will, as long as we walk this earth, need to pay careful attention to the affections, desires, and motives of our hearts. It is why we need the grace of God to change our hearts and the expressions that come from within. Yet God's transformative power can set our hearts free to live with a posture that has an incredible and lasting impact on all those we lead.

You may not consider yourself a leader in a sense of feeling called. However, if you are a man and married you are called to lead your spouse. If you have been blessed with children, make no mistake you are called to lead your children. This call comes from God. If you are a church leader, you are called to lead and shepherd Christ's church. If God has placed you in a leadership position in the workplace He has a mission in mind. I pray you sense the seriousness of this call to lead. The call of God to lead alone should drive us to places to learn and grow. Many of us provide a measure of leadership in aspects we never consider important and consequential. Yet any committee, sports team, department, or activity has the potential to be a place where you can have a significant impact on people's lives. So, with that in mind, journey with me in learning and growing in that divine call.

Cultivate a servant's posture.

To begin to process God's calling on your life to lead let us look at the first posture required. Leadership is many things, and, in my eyes, servanthood is at the core. John Maxwell often states" leadership is influence". I agree. The issue is whether that influence is lasting or fleeting. There can be no deep or lasting influence without servanthood. Servanthood is birthed by grace and is part of what cultivates depth in us. Intentionality in serving is what draws out of that depth. The best leaders are marked by humility and a reflective life.

Jesus is the greatest leader ever and his model of servanthood is a must for us to seek to emulate. In the Gospel of John chapter 13 after washing the disciples' feet, we read these words from Jesus.

"When He had washed their feet and put on His outer garments and resumed His place, he said to them, "Do you understand what I have done for you? You call me Teacher and Lord, and you are right, for so I am. If I then, your Lord and Teacher, have washed your feet, you also ought to wash one another's feet. For I have given you an example, that you also should do just as I have done to you."

John 13:12-15 (ESV)

William Barclay wrote about this scene and its implications,

When we are thinking of our dignity, our prestige, our rights, let us see again the picture of the Son of God, girt with towel, kneeling at His disciples' feet."

The greatest leader gave the key to His leadership. It wasn't power, control, affluence, or excellence in organization but servanthood. A posture of serving others right where they are at. If you are not serving those who you are seeking to lead whether your spouse, children, team, or organization, your influence and impact will quickly plateau and begin to deteriorate. I can quickly identify times I have not served with a posture of servanthood. I recall with regret grace was not fueling my service. In each case, I prioritized outcomes and plans over people. I talked more and listened less. I sought to control, gain buy-in, and shut down concerns and opinions. I am embarrassed and humbled just reflecting on some of those times. In some instances, my failure to serve was tied to the hurt I experienced. Instead of serving those who hurt me I dug in and excused my actions. That is far from Jesus' model. In the upper room, he washed all twelve of the apostles' feet. That included Judas, who would betray him within hours. He knew Judas would betray Him and still He served. The call to lead with Jesus' style of servanthood is not easy. Our sinful inclinations will seek to draw us to selfish agendas.

I have been blessed to have good models of leadership in my life. District leaders like Ken Moberg, Rob Weise, and Don Price. Who model a servant's heart and speak into my life to this day. Fellow elders who were strong leaders and effective because they had a servant's posture. Men like Mick Shilts, Jerry Miller, Tom Nelson, Ken Ness, Bob Rohland, Cary Linder, Dwayne Borg, Eric Wiggins, and others.

These names you probably do not know but I mention them because of how they poured into my life and because their posture provided me a model and visual reminder of servanthood. I am grateful for these men in my life. I need men like these in my life. As I think of how they demonstrated servanthood it occurred to me they share common characteristics. These men were available, approachable, and followed up in a timely manner. They were patient with me as their pastor. They served me by telling me the truth, not to secure my support or further another agenda. I know they prayed, and I am sure still do, for me and my family. They are all generous and express gratitude regularly. They remind me servanthood is demonstrated in many little ways. Because I have had the privilege to serve close to them, I can tell you it wasn't just a public facade. They served that way in their homes. Their example follows throughout my life.

Many leaders in the Christian arena run the risk of being indistinguishable from leaders in the secular arena. The question as to whether our leadership is centered around God or ourselves requires careful reflection and heart analysis of how we serve. Our influence actually can become His influence through us as we serve.

The servant is one whose life and interactions are marked by humility. When we lead in this posture, we seek not immediate results, but we lean into Christ and those practices that take us deeper in our relationship with God. Humility produces strength in character yet is not soft. Like Jesus, a servant is passionate about the things that matter. Servants are uncomfortable being noticed. They are satisfied if they serve in a way where no one sees or knows their name.

Yet it is within us to want control. We can be deceived into thinking our way is best and people should get on board with that. Too often we want the limelight and applause. Seldom desiring others get applause instead. We are slow to celebrate others' successes and quick to speak of ours. We too can slip into thinking others are there to serve us. Humble, servant-hearted leadership enables us to show vulnerability and in so doing invites others to do the same. When we do, we inspire others to be honest and loyal to themselves and others. Serving others also motivates others to tackle their goals with similar energy you use to tackle yours.

What's more, when we as leaders embrace humility, we're more likely to make decisions that have the most impact on others because it's not coming from a place of ego.

Overall, servanthood is not about being insecure or appearing weak. It is a chance to be authentic, helpful, and encouraging to everyone around you. What's more, humble leaders stand out among their peers because they are able to inspire and motivate without using intimidation.

Leadership can be selfish without appearing to be so. There are deeper and more subtle expressions of self-interest that sabotage us from real servanthood. One of these subtle expressions is the tendency for leaders to work out their own insecurities in the midst of their leadership. For example,

- A leader who fears the opinion of others may use leadership to be liked.
- A leader who fears uncertainty may use leadership in order to gain control.
- A leader who fears vulnerability may use leadership as a way to "perform" in front of others and avoid being vulnerable.
- A leader who fears making mistakes may use leadership as a way to avoid risk.

The need to reflect often regarding this area is important. Consider these questions,

What am I most afraid of as a leader?
What do I seek to avoid in the contexts I lead?
What makes me angry? Sad?
What must I as a leader have in order to be satisfied?

I would encourage you to reflect for a moment and write your answers to those questions now. Now, looking at your answers. Can you see ways you are using your leadership for selfish means? Or to seek relief from the fears, doubts, and insecurities you may face?

Do you see yourself posturing in ways that pretend you're something you are not? Are you performing? Maybe you feel the need to work hard to feel acceptable to God, parents, or others. Is there a sense of panic that has you rushing and anxious instead of depending on God? Are you passive leaving others to do jobs you feel are beneath you as a leader?

As selfishness and pride emerge confess those to God and invite Him to create in you a humble and contrite spirit that will enable you to strengthen a posture of servanthood.

We live in a time where demands on leaders are weighty. There seldom seems like enough time. With daytimers packed, we can live in a robotic fashion. This creates tension within those who want to lead with deep influence. Leaders who lead in such a way that impacts others at deep levels lead differently. They prioritize differently. They think differently. They steward time and resources differently. They respond differently. They understand deep impact must be nurtured. They think long term rather than short term. Their posture of serving helps others realize that life is not about them either. Their life's witness and impact are much bigger than themselves. Jesus' disciples needed the reminder that leaders don't seek others to serve them. His words cut to the heart in Luke 22:25-27

> "Jesus *said to them, "The kings of the Gentiles lord it over them; and those who exercise authority over them call themselves benefactors. But you are not to be like that. Instead, the greatest among you should be like the youngest, and the one who rules like the one who serves. For who is greater, the one who is at the table or the one who serves? Is it not the one who is at the table? But I am among you as one who serves.* (NIV)

Jesus' words reveal that servant leadership is counterintuitive to the culture around us. I am guilty of all the shallow experiences and expressions in my efforts to lead. However, Jesus speaks to me through His life and calls me to a posture of servanthood. God brings to mind historical, contemporary, and personal models who show me the way up is down. They taught me if I want to lead, I must grab the towel, wash feet, and love hard. For servanthood starts in the heart and thus undergirds the other factors I will address.

I'd like you to reflect on this question, If those around you were to characterize your attitude and actions as a leader, would they say, "He/She has a servant's heart?" In other words, is your leadership as a husband, dad, or supervisor marked by a sincere desire to help others improve and succeed?

In God's Kingdom, every leader carries the identity of a servant, and any leader who thinks of himself in any other way is in danger of abandoning their true calling. Leaders who do not serve will have no deep or lasting impact. Whereas serving others selflessly results in a deepening influence.

Develop an Authentic Posture

Being "normal" is being the real you that God created you to be. That is who your family needs! The more aligned we are with who God created us to be the greater our leadership will be.[1]

If you are familiar with my first book, *A Normal Guy*, this posture of authenticity will not surprise you. You maximize your leadership by living out your normal self, that is your natural style. I have taken many self-inventories to better understand my own unique, God-given strengths, as well as how to blend and appreciate differences in my home, workplace, and ministry.

Proverbs 16:16 says, *"It is better to gain wisdom than gold. And gaining understanding is better than silver."* (NIV)

According to the author of Proverbs, gaining understanding is of great value. Seeking to understand yourself is both wise and freeing. I encourage you to take some time and clarify your natural and normal style. It can take some time to get comfortable in your own skin.

I took an assessment years ago with the American Association of Christian Counseling[2] and here is what they concluded after I took the evaluation.

"Matthew is often considered daring, bold, and gutsy. He is a risk-taker who likes to be seen as an individualist, not because of versatility but rather because of his determination to succeed. He seeks his own solutions to problems. He displays a high energy factor and is optimistic about the results he can achieve. The word "can't" is not in his vocabulary.... He embraces visions not always seen by others."

So far sounds good. However, there is another side to this as seen in these comments from the evaluator.

"He should realize at times he needs to think a project through, beginning to end before starting the project. Sometimes he becomes emotionally involved in the decision-making process... Sometimes he is so opinionated about a particular problem that he has difficulty letting others participate in the process. He is decisive and prefers to work with decisive leaders. He can experience stress if his leader does not possess similar traits. If pressured his true feelings may emerge."

That evaluation is pretty accurate and other assessments I've taken align pretty closely. Being authentic allows me to build on my strengths and be intentional in working on my weaknesses. As you read above, I have several things I need to consistently work on. I have been told I have a strong leadership presence. This is not always good as I have heard by some I am intimidating. I find it hard to believe but I come off that way to others. My daughters say they are hesitant to introduce their boyfriends to me. To be honest, in that case, I want to be intimidating. But as I honestly look at myself, I can see how some personality types could think that. There is a need to be aware of this when interacting with others. Even more, allow that awareness to lead to choosing a way of relating that helps others feel welcomed and cared for.

John Maxwell has written a book *The Five Levels of Leadership*. And according to Maxwell, they are:

Position – here people follow because they have to. Here your influence will extend no farther than your job description.

Permission – here people follow because they want to. People will follow you beyond your stated authority. This level allows work to be fun. Here if stay too long will level out any continued influence.

Production – Here people follow because of what you have done for the organization. Here success is sensed by many. There is momentum here which allows problems to be fixed. Caution here is that if production suffers there can become a waning influence.

People development – here people follow because of what you have done for them. Here long-range growth appears. One's commitment to developing leaders will ensure ongoing growth to the organization and its people. Great influence at this level.

Personhood – here people follow because of who you are and what you represent. This step is reserved for leaders who have spent years growing people and organizations. Few make it. Those who do have an amazing influence far beyond their life on earth.[3]

Personhood is where I want to be in my leadership. I get excited about the prospect of having a positive influence beyond my years here on earth. It takes growth to move on to each level Maxwell refers to and with each level comes greater impact. I can't help but notice how leading from your authentic self, which I call one's normal, is where the greatest impact will be. I believe when you live according to your normal the impact is extraordinary.

Insecure leaders no matter what the context feel a need to have all the answers and have it all together. When the façade does not match reality anxiety abounds. Leaders who serve do not feel the need to have all the answers. As a matter of fact, they serve by bringing people together to discover the answers.

The authentic leader's self-disclosure invites others' self-disclosure. This allows a realness that produces an atmosphere, an open culture, that makes honest and real dialogue possible. People relate to authenticity. Posturing and a manufactured front appeal to no one. Be a leader who is real more than right.

The authentic leader remains open to correction and accountability. An authentic leader is not afraid of exposure because there is a belief that nothing could be known or exposed that has not already been addressed by the work of the grace of God in our lives. Authentic leaders know that as long as sin still resides in them, they still need to be rescued. Rescued from themselves and their sinful inclination to jostle for position. They need to be delivered from their craving to control rather than serve. Authentic leaders know the danger of sin and the ongoing need for God's grace to restrain and equip us. Every leader must be aware that everyone around them is still in need of that same grace. Deep influence comes from living out of your authentic self.

Authenticity includes transparency. Our lack of transparency can prevent us from connecting with others from understanding us and learning from us. Living authentically involves a transparency where hiding is no longer comfortable because we are growing confident in who God made us and who we are becoming by His grace.

Authenticity protects you and me from living a life of lies. God rewards those who are honest and have a humble heart. Pursue living authentically and start on the inside, before God.

Living authentically is a celebration of who God created you to be. Pursue consistency in being genuine. It has taken me a long time to get comfortable in my skin, but I am in a much better place. When living with authenticity, I am driven by a passion for life and for others. When I live with a false front, I am left to the shallowness of performing.

The following honest prayer reveals what it looks like to get serious about transformation being at the core of moving to a deeper and genuine life.

O persistent God,
deliver me from assuming your mercy is gentle.
Pressure me that I may grow more human,
not through the lessening of my struggles, but through an expansion of them...
Deepen my hurt until I learn to share it and myself openly,
and my needs honestly.
Sharpen my fears until I name themselves and release the power I have locked in them
and they in me.
Accentuate my confusion
until I shed those grandiose expectations
that divert me from the small, glad gifts
of the now and the here and the me.
Expose my shame where it shivers,
crouched behind the curtains of propriety,
until I can laugh at last
through my common frailties and failures,
laugh my way toward becoming whole.[4]

When grace grips you, you are free to be honest and vulnerable. Deep influence is possible when we live transparent lives.

Lead from the Rooftop

My dad was many things but a climber he was not. He did not like heights and was constantly taking jobs and offering favors that required someone to climb on a roof, tall antenna towers, or trees. Guess who actually did the climbing on these jobs. I am not a fan of heights, but I was the guy to climb. One time however we had to fix something on our roof, and it took both of us to complete the job. When we were done, we sat at the peak of the roof and looked over our property. Dad said while he didn't like to climb on the roof, when he did he took the time to sit and look at the property from above. He said when you look at your property from a different perspective you get a better sense of its condition. Gutters that look fine from below when viewed from above may reveal rusting within. Looking down at the garage roof may reveal the shingles are cracking. Dying branches in trees not seen from below may be visible from the perspective of the roof. I learned that day on the peak of our house roof that the true condition of your property is best scene from the rooftop. Likewise, the true condition of our leadership is often seen from a different perspective. That is the perspective from above. God enables us to see the true condition of our leadership from above in the Bible. The Bible gives us a heavenly view of how to best lead. We receive the best view possible and that is from God's perspective. When it comes to leadership it is the condition of our hearts which matters most.

I believe the idea of seeing things from a different perspective in regard to leading others is of great value. If you want to see the true condition of your marriage, children, home, team, staff or department learn to see it from the expressions of your heart. From the inside out. Leading from the rooftop means we look deep within and gauge our leadership by the flow of grace as seen in servanthood and authenticity. There is great freedom that results from seeing our leadership from a different perspective. The perspective of the Bible, friends, evaluations, family members, and coworkers all can bear great fruit.

From the surface circumstances that reveal our failures when viewed from a different perspective may show we no longer need to fear failure. Times we thought we let others down from the perspective above showed we no longer need to be weighed down by expectations. Once we see ourselves in need of forgiveness and strength, from a different perspective we see in Christ He has already offered these things. When all we can see are our sinful inclinations when we look from a different perspective we see that Jesus washes us with grace. From the rooftop we learn repentance is an avenue to a deeper experience of His grace. On the rooftop, it's the posture of servanthood and authenticity that reveals, brings and positions us for deep change.

CHAPTER TWO

Leading Yourself

Within all contexts of leadership, leading oneself is critical. Leading oneself implies intentionality. Intentional choices, priorities, standards, and boundaries to name a few. Critical choices we make about attitudes, disciplines, emotions, and speech comprise our character and will determine the degree of good we have in regard to influencing others. We need a change in our hearts, priorities, thinking, and our relationships. Knowing that is easier than initiating and pursuing change. How do we lead ourselves toward that change? Let's consider practices that are grace dependent.

The Attitude of a Leader

The dictionary defines attitude as *a manner, disposition, feeling, or position with regard to a person or thing, a tendency or orientation of the mind.*

Simply put, it's the posture that you choose to approach life in general.

Attitude is the way you mentally look at the world around you. It is how you view your current environment and your future. It is an aspect of developing one's worldview. Consider these questions.

- Does life suck, and then you die?
- Is life a meaningful journey filled with hope?
- Is life meaningless, and by extension everything you do?
- Is God involved with my life?

How you answer these questions becomes the lens through which you view life. By your attitudes you see the world. Besides the part they play in developing a worldview; we have our attitudes toward other details. For instance, like work, is it a chore or a joy? Are the problems we face a challenge or a dead end? Relationships are they a joy or pain? In the case of leadership is it a chore or opportunity?

Attitudes can be broadly categorized as positive or negative. Positive attitudes are those that promote growth, development, and collaboration, while negative attitudes hinder progress and create a toxic environment.

Positive attitudes include optimism, hope, belief, enthusiasm, and gratitude.

Optimism is the belief that things will turn out well, even in the face of adversity. Optimistic leaders believe and inspire those they lead to overcome obstacles, stay motivated, and pursue their goals, even in challenging circumstances. If you don't feel this is important, I encourage you to coach a middle school team. While this is true in any business, home, team, church, or organization in my experience over the years the middle school level is where I see the greatest correlation. There is noticeable effort and enthusiasm which results when hope and optimism are pumped into these kids. Some words connected to a positive attitude are hope, belief, enthusiasm, and gratefulness.

Hope is the expectation of a positive outcome even when it looks dim and there is no way to move forward. Leaders who are purveyors of hope create a sense and belief of possibility which inspires greater creativity and innovation.

Belief is the conviction that something is true. Leaders who believe in themselves and their team members can inspire confidence and a sense of purpose. The motivation that can come from the words "I believe in you" is off the charts.

Enthusiasm is the passion and energy that comes from serving in your sweet spot which is simply doing something that one loves. Leaders who approach their work with enthusiasm can inspire those they lead to do the same. This can lead to greater engagement and accomplishment. I know when I had the kids help me with chores, I tried to make it fun so they could see it is possible to enthusiastically go about even the most mundane tasks. Just ask them how much fun we had going to the dump.

Gratitude is the intentional practice of acknowledging and appreciating the many good things around us. Leaders who cultivate gratitude in themselves and others add great value to all.

We also must be aware of negative attitudes that may mentally challenge us at any given moment. I would consider attitudes such as pessimism, doubt, fear, ego, and a sense of entitlement as enemies of successful and fruitful leaders. I cannot think of one good thing that comes from negativity. Not one.

We must continually evaluate our attitudes. We must never underestimate or excuse them. Chuck Swindoll's words regularly remind me of the importance of my attitude.

"The longer I live, the more I realize the impact of attitude on life. Attitude, to me, is more important than facts. It is more important than the past, than education, than money, than circumstances, than failure, than successes, than what other people think or say or do. It is more important than appearance, giftedness, or skill. It will make or break a company. . . a person. . . a home. The remarkable thing is we have a choice every day regarding the attitude we will embrace for that day. We cannot change our past. . we cannot change how other people will act. The only thing we can do is play on the one thing we have, and that is our attitude. . . I am convinced that life is 10% what happens to me and 90% how I react to it. And so it is with you. . . we are in charge of our attitude."

It must be emphasized again. The success of your leadership in the home or organization is most dependent on your attitude. If you are a leader, the good news is, you can make that choice. You have a choice each day and, in each interaction, to choose a positive attitude toward the people you're leading. You have a choice to push away the attitudes that think the worst about people and circumstances. Along with our attitudes towards people; our attitudes toward life will make all the difference as well.

As a leader, you'll be facing a lot of challenges. An internal struggle like a conflict at home or the workplace or an external challenge that is testing the success and survivability of your organization.

It is ultimately your attitude that will make all the difference in whether you're successful in tackling the challenges. In leadership, we must constantly be aware of the things that are influencing us. Although you are constantly influencing people, you yourself are constantly being influenced by your surroundings.

Awareness becomes key: What is in your surroundings? What are the books you read? People you speak to? Online content you consume? Social media like Facebook and Twitter are generally negative. People complain, accuse, and lay blame under the veil of anonymity. If you spend long enough on social media, it won't be a surprise when negativity, anger, and dissatisfaction surface.

If you hang out regularly with negative people, you will be influenced unconsciously. Your mindset will look for ways to be unhappy. Negative people are joy and optimism suckers. Like it or not, all these things influence your thinking and your attitudes. Think of the five closest people to you and often your attitude is affected by them far more than you realize. So be careful about what and who you allow around yourself; these factors unconsciously shape your attitudes.

As I read about the apostle Paul's life, he seemed to have a hard edge and was at times brutally honest. What is most clear to me is his healthy attitude. It allowed him to serve the way He did and have the impact he did. One example is found in this passage.

Brethren, I count not myself to have apprehended: but this one thing I do, forgetting those things which are behind, and reaching forth unto those things which are before, I press toward the mark for the prize of the high calling of God in Christ Jesus. Philippians 3:13-14

His attitude allowed him to forget that which could hinder him. His attitude allowed him to press on to fulfill what God had called him to. Like Paul, leaders need to consistently choose an attitude that sets them free to be all that God desires.

Consider the tasks a leader in the marketplace is responsible for carrying out each day. Responsibilities such as organization, decision-making, problem-solving, planning, conflict resolution, staff evaluations, team meetings, and the list goes on. In each of these, the leader's attitude determines the success of these efforts. I would strongly encourage you to slow down enough during your day and evaluate whether your attitude is right to engage in the task. If you discern your attitude needs adjustment, take a few moments and ask God to help you operate with a healthy attitude.

The disciplines of a leader

When it comes to personal disciplines it is obvious, but it must be said, 'No one can do these for you". Developing consistency in growth requires self-leadership. When I speak of disciplines, I am referring to consistent habits that bring growth. Disciplines that open our hearts and minds to God's Word and the flow of His grace. Personal disciplines are like vitamins that show no daily benefits but over longer periods of time bring health to one's heart, mind and body.

- **Bible Reading, prayer, and reflection**

These are disciplines that have borne great fruit in my life. I can confidently say that these have been the source of whatever growth has taken place in my life.

A remarkable aspect of God's design of us is that we have the ability to pause and reflect, to think and apply truth. We can discern what God is doing over what others may be doing. If we were being honest, and we must be to have a deep influence, we can admit our minds and thoughts get fragmented. Text notifications, tweets, video ads, and clips seem to have eroded our capacity for meaningful attention. How do we address this inability to think about what really matters? Make the Bible where you start. Make God's voice the first thing you hear each day. Let His voice through the Scriptures speak life into your spirit. Read His words with unhurried reflection in the morning and the place you regain focus during the day. Aim to have His word be "upon your heart" and central in your marriage, parenting, and other contexts of leading. You will discover over time God can rebuild your mind and restore your heart.

By faith, I know God's Word and His Spirit are producing in me the righteous life He desires. The Bible gives me the perspective, wisdom, and clarity I need each day. To neglect these disciplines is to limit severely the positive development of my wife, children, and teams or groups I may lead.

I have many journals I have written over the years that I revisit and reread to remind me of God's work in my life and the lessons He has taught me—lessons that He wants me to continue to apply today.

These journals record reflections on what God has taught me over the years through the Bible, circumstances, and people. My journals speak to God's grace operating in my life over and over. Pages full of confessions, at times deep hurt, concerns, grief, and disappointments. Greater than all of that is how God met me with His gracious presence. Perhaps you have not created space for the discipline of reading the Bible and praying. Let me encourage you. You do not need to read much each day, but you do need to think about it and perhaps write down what you learn. This discipline will allow you to look back on your days and see the hand of God like no other discipline.

The Bible teaches that when someone trusts Christ as their Savior, God gives His Spirit to indwell that person. I can testify to the Spirit's encouragement, conviction, leadership, and voice in my life. The Holy Spirit enables me to see what lies beneath the surface of my life. The entries in my journal form a composite of who I once was and who I am now in the process of becoming. The Holy Spirit helps me see what I need to see. There were things I didn't see in the past, and now, as I look back at what I have learned, they seem obvious. In short, I see God's grace at work.

If this has not been one of your disciplines, I encourage you to find a Bible reading plan and spend even fifteen minutes reading and thinking about what you read. I've encouraged many who have begun this discipline to start in the Gospel of John. Next, spend time making a prayer list of people and situations that you care about. Start by spending a couple of minutes talking to God about helping those on your list and their requests. Like I discovered along with your prayer list write down whatever strikes you from reading or a situation or encounter you had that impacted you.

These disciplines will help you lead those you love like nothing else.

- **Develop a personal mission**.

I want to strongly encourage you to spend some time thinking through what God wants you to do with your time on earth and who He wants you to invest in. This is the beginning of gaining clarity on how you will invest your time and energy. This discipline is a process.

Some questions to process to get you started are:

- What are the core convictions God has given you?
- Who has God specifically called you to invest in?
- What circumstances in your life have had the most impact and why?

All these questions can help you process and develop a mission statement for your life. I crafted my personal mission over much reflection on Scripture, personal evaluation of passions, convictions, and impacting circumstances and persons God has brought into my life to name a few factors. I have tweaked it over the years as God refined His call to my heart. I have my personal mission posted in my office and read this regularly. This serves as a great aid in me eliminating pursuits or plans that squeeze my energy and time from pursuing God's call on my life. I have included my personal mission below for you to have an idea of how clarifying this can be for your life.

My Personal Mission

I live to bring glory to Almighty God by the worship of who He is, by an authentic faith, and lifestyle that reflects God's grace and truth, and by giving myself to His calling in my life.

God has specifically called me to:

- To my Savior and a growing intimacy with Him.
- To my wife, Cyndy. To cherish her and serve her. To help her discover her giftedness and her role in ministry and to build her up.
- To my children. To love them and lead them to follow Jesus. To leave a legacy for them to live and pass on. A legacy marked by active faith in Christ, compassion, humility, integrity, and faithfulness.
- To my brothers and sisters in Christ. To model for and encourage them into a deeper walk with Christ. To encourage them to give their lives for the Kingdom of God by helping them discover and use their God-given gifts and passions.
- To pray for and mentor a new generation of leaders.
- To my world. To pray for and proclaim the good news of Jesus Christ. My mission field begins at home and then to my sphere of influence, community and to extend in increasing measure.

It is one thing to write up a mission for your life but believe me another to live it out day to day. Yet without clarity on how you will live your life all the activities and demands can lead to a driftless, draining, and fruitless life. It is easy to be involved with many things and have no impact on any one thing. The clarity of a personal mission brings a conviction that what we do really matters. That's how we live and love can even have eternal consequences.

The lack of a compelling mission will cause frustration and can suck the life out of our activities. Do you have a mission worth living for? Is there a passion and drive placed deep within you that begs to be expressed? These passions and convictions are grace gifts from the Holy Spirit. It takes you spending time before God, His Word, and personal evaluation to bring this clarity. You cannot lead others into their mission without knowing yours. You cannot have a deep influence without clarifying the direction that influence is most likely to occur.

The emotions of a leader

Choosing a healthy and positive attitude and incorporating key disciplines position you to experience the gracious presence of Jesus. To lead yourself well also will require you to learn how to navigate emotions. Emotions are unique in that they are both dumb and powerful. I don't mean dumb in that God created something that is worthless or indifferent. But they often aren't based on truth or falsehood they just are. If you have daughters, you may have heard from them with tears in their eyes 'I don't know why I am crying'. Or your spouse may be late, and you get angry at their insensitivity only to find their delay was due to a flat tire. Your anger acted upon falsehood and in that, your emotion of anger was void of reason. Whether leading your marriage, your children, or teams you will experience a full array of emotions. Sadness, fear, surprise, anger, disgust. Take your pick.

You will need to give direction to your emotions, or they will sidetrack you. Many have in a moment of unchecked extreme emotion have undercut efforts they have made and halted momentum that had been built in their life, family, or business. Directing your emotions may seem strange to you, however, if you don't, they will direct you. Leaders in whatever contexts carry an even greater responsibility in this area.

Wisconsin is a beautiful state to live in and summer brings beautiful weather and green fields, lawns, and trees. If you don't like the color green you may need to choose another place to live. The hobby farm my wife and I live on has some pasture for the horses we own. (I am seeking to be a good husband, so I said "we") With pastures and horses comes fencing. We were out early this summer putting a fence around the lower pasture and when we were finished and came inside, we knew we had to check our clothes and skin for ticks. These little bugs can bring lymes disease and are simply a nuisance. Ticks don't simply visit you they latch on to you and if not dealt with can cause problems. There are some emotions if they attach themselves to you for any length of time can cause real problems. It is easy to ignore negative emotions as a leader as we feel the need to always be "on our game'. When emotions get ignored and pent up, they almost always come out in destructive ways.

I find fear, despair, and anger as the big three when it comes to what leaders deal with. These three emotions are like ticks that when attached to you make it difficult to grow. They can hinder the work of grace in our hearts. Of course, some emotions can be good at times. Fear of being mauled by a bear can cause you to keep your distance. Anger at the violence and evil around us is fitting and not problematic. However, these seem to be less in our experiences than the negative expressions. Let's take a look at these big three.

Fear of disappointing someone, fear of health, failure, or judgement can cripple and steal one's confidence. Fear can also cause a leader to hesitate to do the right things. What overcomes fear is grace. The grace of God toward you and the work of grace within you.

I played college baseball for one year. I was a pitcher and had modest success in high school, so I thought I'd give it a whirl. I had a decent fastball and curveball. I remember coming into my first game and having a clean inning. Three batters up and three down. I came into pitch the next game and hung a curve ball, and the batter crushed it. I think it still hasn't landed. That one hit created a fear of failure in me. I struggled to believe I had what it took to pitch in college baseball. I finished the year and had some okay moments but to this day I still can picture the pitch and the long homerun. In retrospect, I wasn't good enough anyway, but it was fear that created the initial roadblock toward improvement. What had really happened was that the fear of failure stole my confidence. Worse yet it blocked the work of grace.

Evaluate the fear-producing situation in your life and deal with one aspect of it at a time. Break the situation down into smaller pieces and attack one at a time. Resist the temptation to make decisions based on fear and instead make them based on faith. Each time you conquer a small piece of what is causing you fear confidence begins to build up. Simply put instead of running because of fear, attack it by faith.

Despair is another emotion that can attach itself to you rendering you ineffective. Despair which you could also call discouragement is like a wet blanket over you and your situation. While it may not shut down someone like fear is capable of doing, discouragement over the long haul can suck the life out of a leader, bring distorted perspective, steal joy, and lead to depression. To make matters worse it could also spread to the people you may be seeking to lead. Misery does love company.

The key to not letting despair attach to you is to spend time with positive and mature people. In my leadership experiences as a pastor, I have been blessed to have served with positive people. Yes, there were some I served with who I would categorize as negative and were hindered by fear, despair, or anger. I chose to draw near to those who helped me keep focused on moving forward in faith. Don Price was a pastor who invested in my life and who helped me process God's call on my life. He has throughout my life been a great encouragement.

When I served as the Senior Pastor in Sparta, Wisconsin years ago, we called a new youth pastor to come to serve. His name is Nate Palmer, and he has such a welcoming and positive nature about him. During some of the tough times in serving there, he was a great help to me in keeping my focus and optimism. Hard meetings and tension were not as difficult to work through when I had a team member who helped me stay positive and focused.

There simply is no way around it times of discouragement will come and the best way to deal with them is to be prepared for them. You cannot lead others under a pile of discouragement. Like going to a gas station to fill up your gas tank go get a fill up from friends who will listen and steer you back toward an optimistic and productive mindset.

Anger is another emotion that when attached to us can lead to stifling any growth or impact. Is it just me or is a tsunami of anger spreading over our culture? Road rage, sports rage, social media rage, marital rage, political outrage, and children out of control. It seems everyone is ready to explode in anger over something. It wouldn't be nearly as problematic if anger was channeled into something positive, but it takes destructive forms.

Due to the pressure, tension and sheer energy it takes to lead is it no wonder anger begins to emerge in so many marriages, homes, and workplaces. It is helpful to consider the most common causes of anger.

- Learned behavior
- Betrayal
- Feeling wronged
- Being put down
- Stress and pressure
- Unmet needs or expectations
- Disrespect
- Physical issues

- Rebellion

Counselor and Author Tim Clinton agrees anger is a severe problem today.

Many live in a cage of anger in the confines of their own homes. Anger in America's marriages is exploding off the chart. The same thing goes for anger in the workplace. We know that children who live in home-based cages of anger grow up to produce the same environment in their adult lives.[1]

Listen to a few passages from the Bible that hit on the danger of anger and its effect on one's growth.

Proverbs 14:29 (NLT): *"People with understanding control their anger; a hot temper shows great foolishness."*

James 1:20 (ESV) *"For the anger of man does not produce the righteousness of God."*

Ephesians 4:26 (ESV) *"Be angry and do not sin; do not let the sun go down on your anger"*

Proverbs 29:11 (ESV) *"A fool gives full vent to his spirit, but a wise man quietly holds it back"*

Ecclesiastes 7:9 (ESV) *"Be not quick in your spirit to become angry, for anger lodges in the heart of fools."*

The above passages alone tell us anger is foolish and produces nothing good. The words, "anger lodges in the heart" seen in the Ecclesiastes passage are especially sobering. You cannot have anger lodged in one's heart and grace operating out of the same heart at the same time. Unmanaged anger will rob a leader of growth and severely limit the development of other leaders. Anger continues to bring so much damage to marriages, friendships, homes, churches, and organizations. Solomon, the author of Proverbs, affirms the value of controlling one's anger in Proverbs 16:32

Whoever is slow to anger is better than the mighty,
 and he who rules his spirit than he who takes a city. (ESV)

Proverbs 16:32 teaches us that controlling your anger is more important than your leadership plans, principles, and strategies.

The Bible is so relevant and provides teaching on how to live in practical ways and that is certainly true in regard to this issue. I want to leave you with some help to move past what could ambush your progress.

I was reading Psalm 4:4 and discovered this insight. It jumps out even more when we look at three translations next to each other. Observe the second part of the verse.

In your anger do not sin, when you are on your beds, search your hearts and be silent. (NIV)
Don't sin by letting anger control you. Think about it overnight and remain silent." (NLT)
Be angry, and do not sin; ponder in your own hearts on your beds and be silent. (ESV)

The verses reveal a key to dealing with anger. That is to remove yourself from the problem or situation. In this case, the Psalmist went to his home and allowed God to search him and reveal the truth to him throughout the night. He removed himself from the anger-inducing circumstances and thought it through. This is not a rehearsing or rehashing of what caused the anger but a searching of one's own heart. Whether it is a goal of yours being blocked or an idol being threatened ask God to reveal the condition of your heart. Life-changing counsel is found in this Psalm.

Perhaps it is time to get on the rooftop and pay attention to your emotions! Emotionally unhealthy leaders cannot lead those they love well and potentially may bring hurt upon them.

The speech of a leader

Limited skills and productivity can hinder you and slow you down, but a lack of character will eventually halt any progress. If you lack ability or skill, you can improve but if you lack character you are headed for heartbreak. Character is clearly reflected in our speech. When the emotion of anger is present the volatility magnifies in our speech. Jesus made a significant connection when speaking to a group of religious leaders. He said:

> *You brood of vipers! How can you speak good, when you are evil? For out of the abundance of the heart the mouth speaks.* Matthew 12:34 (ESV)

Here is the connection if we want to have a lasting and deep impact, that is one which flows out of the work of grace in our hearts, then we must address speech that Jesus says flows out of our hearts.

When we look all around God's creation, we see that only human beings have the ability to communicate through the spoken word. The ability to use words is a unique and powerful gift from God. The Bible shows us, again and again, a connection between our hearts and our mouths. I think many miss this connection. When we pursue living authentically and leading others we must pay attention to our words. Our words not only reveal what's in the heart, but our words also affirm the authenticity of our leadership. If we are serious about becoming who God wants us to be, we won't want to ignore this area of our lives. The writer of Proverbs tells us, "The tongue has the power of life and death, and those who love it will eat its fruit" (Proverbs 18:21 ESV).

Words are not simply sounds caused by air passing through our larynx. Words do more than convey information. Words can destroy one's spirit and even stir up hatred and violence. They can inflict wounds or worsen them. Make no mistake—words have power!

In light of the power of words, a key question for every one of us is: "Are we using words to build up people or bring harm to them?" Are our words filled with hate or love, bitterness or blessing, complaining or compliments?

I have done a fair amount of pre-marital counseling for engaged couples over the years. Time and time again, I have seen couples amazed at the amount of Bible passages that speak to what and how we communicate. Here are just a few passages.

"The mouth of the righteous produces' wisdom, but a perverse tongue will be cut out. The lips of the righteous know what is appropriate, but the mouth of the wicked, only what is perverse."
Proverbs 10:31-32 (ESV)

"A gentle answer turns away anger, but a harsh word stirs up wrath. The tongue of the wise makes knowledge attractive, but the mouths of fools blurt out foolishness." …... The tongue that heals is a tree of life, but a devious tongue breaks the spirit."
Proverbs 15:1-2,4 (ESV)

"A word spoken at the right time is like gold apples in silver settings."
Proverbs 25:11 (ESV)

And perhaps the most descriptive passage on the power of our speech is from the book of James where we read,

"A bit in the mouth of a horse controls the whole horse. A small rudder on a huge ship in the hands of a skilled captain sets a course in the face of the strongest winds. A word out of your mouth may seem of no account, but it can accomplish nearly anything—or destroy it!

It only takes a spark, remember, to set off a forest fire. A careless or wrongly placed word out of your mouth can do that. By our speech, we can ruin someone's day, turn harmony to chaos, throw mud on a reputation, send the atmosphere up in smoke, and go up in smoke with it.

This is scary: You can tame a tiger, but you can't tame a tongue—it's never been done. The tongue runs wild, a wanton killer. With our tongues we bless God our Father; with the same tongues, we curse the very men and women He made in His image. Curses and blessings out of the same mouth!"
James 3:3-10 (MSG)

These few verses make it quite clear that God cares about how we communicate. The above Scripture affirms that we have a choice of how we will speak and there are consequences for what we say. Jesus added even more weight to the seriousness of how we speak when He said,

"But I tell you that every careless word that people speak, they shall give an accounting for it in the Day of Judgment". (Matthew 12:39 NASB)

Our speech is a serious issue. We will be held accountable for how we speak. We must consider this when we evaluate how we interact in all contexts I am addressing. When we are engaging at home, work, school, or anywhere else we will help or hurt others by our words. We will honor them or insult them by our words. If you want to lead well use your words to encourage and not tear down.

Robert Wolgemuth, in his excellent book "The Most Important Place on Earth," says, *"Mouths are loaded guns, and words they speak can be lethal. . . When words are spoken, they're always real. Words are never blanks. They're actual bullets, and their impact is absolute. Every time." It is helpful and challenging to look at our speech as a loaded gun and our words as bullets. When we do, it causes us to evaluate the harm that results from careless words. Words are never blanks; they are always real. They have an impact every time."*[2]

No matter what context you lead in if you want grace to flow into others' lives keep a guard over your speech.

The disciplines of time reading and praying, developing a personal mission statement, managing your emotions, and guarding your speech help us rely on God and create opportunities for deep impact. The longer we engage with these disciplines rhythms develop. These rhythms, like breathing, bear consistent fruit and help us break free from the dangers that hinder having a deep impact. It is through disciplines that we pave the way for greater impact and learn the freedom from destructive habits.

The following chapters, on leading your spouse, and your children are coming from my perspective as a man. Questions I ask myself such as, "As a man how do I love my wife and children in such a way to have a deep impact in their life? While I am sure these thoughts in the next two chapters will be of benefit to all who read them, I have directed them specifically toward husbands and dads.

Leading oneself requires you to view yourself and life through God's lens. God uses persons who seem rather ordinary and insignificant. Yet the commitment of those persons to grow personally can make a huge impact. I came across this quote by Calvin Miller when reading one of my journals recently.

Miller writes, *"Great works of God rarely start in big places. Rather they start in small places – in some person with a big commitment."*

Lead yourself well in your places. Commit to having a deep influence and you can watch God do a great work.

CHAPTER THREE

Leading Your Spouse

Husbands, lead your wife toward being healthy, not happy.

October 12, 1991, I remember that day like yesterday. How could I not? I stood in the front of a large room surrounded by friends and family about to experience a significant event. After several months of counseling, I was about to embark on an incredible journey with a woman named Cyndy. We had prepared as best we could, but I felt both deep gratitude and soberness all at the same time when I saw the most beautiful woman walk down the aisle. As we began this new journey it wasn't long before we embraced the idea that we were to leave the two different normals we carried into the marriage and would now cleave to a new normal-our new normal.

Think of what thoughts and mindsets couples carry into their marriage. The way things were in their homes, their "normals".

Consider this list of possible normals one may have grown up with:

Moms should quit work and stay home when children come.
The fun of Christmas is sleeping in.
No home is complete without a dog.
Dads always do the driving.
Two people who really love each other will never argue.
Being on time is important.
Church on Sundays is optional.
Toothpaste should be squeezed from the middle.

Now imagine the other spouse who may have these normal.
Children should have no bearing on mom's employment.
The fun of Christmas is getting up very early and opening gifts.
No dogs or cats! But a deer mount and a bear rug are fine. (I'm from Wisconsin can you tell?)
Two people who love each other often argue.
Showing up within a half hour is fine

Church on Sunday is non-negotiable.
Squeezing toothpaste – who cares?

The list is endless of what we bring into our marriages. No wonder it requires much time, energy, and above all compromise to find a couple's new normal.

You and I perhaps can look back and smile at the many ways our homes were different from our spouses growing up. Cyndy and I were raised in many different ways. She on a farm in Wisconsin. Me in a city in Illinois. Her parental authority dynamic was the polar opposite of the way I was raised. My family is very affectionate and hers is more reserved. We ate at 5:00 pm virtually every evening. Her family mostly after chores at about 8:00. The list is endless. On that day when we said our vows the creation of our new normal began. Even more stretching than all the differences was that I knew I was called to lead this journey.

I don't know if you have ever thought back to the beginning of creation about the process God used in bringing Adam and Eve together. Here is how Genesis 2:24 tells it. *"A man shall leave his father and his mother and hold fast to his wife, and they shall become one flesh. And the man and his wife were both naked and not ashamed."*

The action words "hold fast" used here can also be translated "cleave". The words are instructive. Both you and your spouse left mom and dad and now hold fast to one another and carry into your marriage normal ways of doing life.

Unfortunately, after Scripture reveals God's design for marriage we also read sin entered the world. We read how the "very good" man became the weak man. Genesis 2-3 tells us there was a serpent in the garden (satan) who deceived the two. Here is how he went about it.

1. The serpent engaged the woman 1st. (attacked God's creation order immediately)
2. The serpent lied about what God had said.
3. The serpent directly counters what God said.
4. The woman followed the serpent's lies.
5. The man passively withdraws.
6. The man walked away from the problem which amplified the problem.

I share this because it teaches us much about the attack on manhood and his leadership in the union with his wife. Consider some of the characteristics of modern manhood and notice how they connect with Adam's actions in Genesis 2-3.

Modern man's main orientation is

- Passive
- Feminine
- Non-confrontational
- Led by feelings, not truth
- No accountability
- Take little on as obligations (especially those related to biblical manhood)
- Other dependent

In contrast, Biblical man's orientation is one of

- Self-sacrificing
- Humility
- Protecting
- Respecting of women
- Leading
- Serving God
- Providing
- Protecting

Read through the lists again considering the effect these have on marriage. It is of the utmost importance we align ourselves with God's design and desires for man if we are to lead our marriages well. We dare not take our cues from the modern view of men. If we do the impact on our marriages will be destructive as society shows us each day.

Parental models, priorities, expectations, traditions, and the list goes on of the differing perspectives you brought into your relationship as husband and wife. God's perspective on the marriage relationship is clear and certainly challenging.

You will need to have a great love for your wife and a greater love still for God. You must be willing to count yourself last. You must be willing to die for your wife but, harder still, to live for her. You need to be willing and equipped to lead your wife/family with a humble, confident, godly love. Scripture provides God's instructions for how the marriage can flourish.

> *Husbands, in the same way be considerate as you live with your wives and treat them with respect as the weaker partner and as heirs with you of the gracious gift of life, so that nothing will hinder your prayers.*
>
> 1 Peter 3:7

God has called husbands to lead their marriage relationship. This is a taboo thought in today's culture marred by feminism. Hopefully, like me, you don't care to listen to the voices of culture. Those voices are both deceptive and destructive. The damaging consequences of the distortion of God's design of man and marriage are on display any time you turn on the TV or click on social media. Thus, leadership in the home is under assault.

I have a deep appreciation for Cyndy's commitment to God's design for the roles of the headship of the husband and the coming alongside (biblical submission) of the wife. She came to trust Jesus Christ as her Savior in high school. She grew up viewing varied ordered marital relationships. When we began dating and then married, she showed a willing commitment to carry out the role God laid out for her in Scripture and follow me in the role God has for me to lead. She has not listened to the voices of culture that cry "submission' is akin to being a doormat.

God's design of marriage provides the best context for leading from a heart of grace. God gives grace to those who do life and marriage His way.

Even though we commit to living aligned to God's design doesn't mean we will always carry it out well. Sin is forever rearing its ugly head and causing disruption and disunity in marriage relationships. That makes living and leading from grace essential.

Whether it's my garage door opener, bicycle or belt pully in my car they all need to be lubricated. Oil reduces the friction and allows smoother functioning. For the friction in marriage, it is grace that is the oil that allows biblical expressions of love and servanthood possible.

I attended a marriage workshop by my friend Chad Eichstadt a couple of years ago, and he shared these five action steps I felt were very practical in inviting authenticity into our marriages. I feel they make possible the free flow of the oil of grace into our marriages. I have added comments underneath each action step.

1. Communicate Your Needs and Wants Out Loud: Talk about Everything

He encouraged communication about day-to-day needs as well as listening to what your wife needs and wants. This cannot be a periodic exercise but a day-to-day commitment.

2. Deal With the Small Things that Undermine Your Relationship

Resentment accumulates if people are unwilling to confront the issues at the outset. Suggestion: feel free to say, "you know what I don't like." Give each other a safe place to be honest and discuss the hard stuff.

3. Quickly and Completely Resolve Conflicts

Many couples will periodically engage in arguments in which each speaks in anger and frustration saying hurtful things. Over time they cool down and life goes on without ever properly resolving the disputes. As the years pass, their marriage is affected by hurts and scars that never heal. Paul vividly warns the Ephesians of the danger lurking behind unresolved conflict.

Be angry and yet do not sin; do not let the sun go down on your anger, and do not give the devil an opportunity." Ephesians 4:26-27 (NIV)

To leave an issue unresolved and to remain angry is like letting the devil into your house to wreak his havoc. Marriages fraught with unresolved conflicts are more vulnerable to increasingly destructive conflicts.

4. Remember Why You Got Married in the First Place

You marry someone because they make you feel good. They bring a fulfillment relationally no one on earth can. The world is antagonistic and chaotic and it's really nice to have someone cheering for you. Both partners need to recognize why they married the other. It also comes down to talking about resentments before they fester. Everyone has bad habits, be it over-criticizing or doing whatever it is that causes the criticism. What matters is how partners handle both and that they remember why they married one another in the first place.

5. Never Stop Paying Attention to the Little Things

Little gestures can go a long way. Acts of service that one does for the other that are completely selfless can build equity in marriage. These ways of expressing love and affection, and attention to another person might tend to slowly slip away because of the understandable stresses that happen in day-to-day living. Invest in caring about the little things.

Chad's principles speak to the necessity of working at your marriage amidst the stresses that distract us from our marriage relationships. Positive small interactions and intentional actions are the glue to a marriage. And when the loving expressions slip relational drift occurs. It is the practical day-to-day actions and relational investments I am called to lead. It is easy to wait for my wife Cyndy to take the first step toward me but that is not what it is to lead. Even though we may take those steps toward our spouses is no guarantee they respond but leading the one you love requires consistent and persistent effort.

There are a couple of convictions that have fueled the action steps I have undertaken to lead Cyndy. I have been far from a perfect husband believe me, but I keep these on my radar to keep or get myself back on track.

Lead your wife toward health

It was about fifteen years ago that God gave me an aha moment. You would think with over fifteen years of marriage I would have figured this out. I can be a slow learner. My focus walking into marriage was to work hard to make Cyndy happy. If she appeared unhappy, I felt I needed to do something, get her something, or create some kind of 'win" for her happiness. Understand she never asked me to do this, and while she does enjoy certain things, I thought I needed to leverage them so she would be happy.

One day in my devotions I was reflecting on the health of the kids. I was evaluating their spiritual and emotional health which I do at times. The question settled in my mind what about Cyndy's health? Then came a thought that has been my focus since that day. My call was not to make Cyndy happy. I am called to help her be healthy. Don't misunderstand I want her to be happy, but I am to lead her to be healthy not happy. It was never my responsibility to scurry around seeking to keep her happy tank full.

Happiness is her choice. A choice I cannot make for her. When all is said and done happiness is not drawn from the deep work of God's grace in a heart. Happiness is often shallow for it is circumstantial dependent. Because I sought her happiness, I avoided what God may have wanted to use to grow her and us.

Your wife's health is something you can contribute to as you live authentically and with a posture of servanthood. I encourage you to intentionally make opportunities available and encourage her to pursue spiritual health as she draws from God's work of grace. God's grace teaches us how to love our wives. Grace opens the door for a deeper intimacy.

Happiness will not take our wives to the places God wants. God wants me to have a deep influence in Cyndy's life and that can only be done if I seek to draw out of the grace at work within me and call her that same work. When the goal is happiness, fear will create avoidance of the hard and challenging conversations and decisions. If happiness is the goal, we may move away from those circumstances God may want to use in our spouses to grow her. If I focus on leading her toward what is healthy, I can live authentically and serve her well bringing stability in our relationship. I have learned healthy creates something deeper than being happy.

Being healthy spiritually, emotionally, and relationally brings something deeper than happiness. It brings joy. Joy transcends circumstances and trials. I do not always do this well and admit frustration when the results of leading toward healthy conversations and pursuits aren't what I envisioned. Maybe you can relate, but we cannot stop seeking the health of our spouses. Many men are running around trying to give their wives everything they want assuming she will be happy only to find out that isn't so. That is the wrong way to lead and will only tire you out and frustrate you. Take it from me.

Seeking to encourage and support her when she is in her 20s looks different when she is in her 50s. Along with the changing seasons in marriage, circumstances you encounter unexpectedly require you as the leader in your home to evaluate and consider her needs to grow more than her wants for happiness.

I find 1 Peter 3:7 very helpful for husbands.

Likewise, husbands, live with your wives in an understanding way, showing honor to the woman as the weaker vessel, since they are heirs with you of the grace of life, so that your prayers may not be hindered.

Two words "Live" and "understanding" jump out at me.

The word "live" carries the idea of aligning yourself with others. Literally, it translates "be down at home with." The term calls for companionship. It speaks to relational closeness. Husbands are you initiating the cultivating of an in-depth partnership? What evidence do you see of a growing companionship? Seeking to build a relational and emotional connection is to lead your wife toward health.

The word "understanding" in 1 Peter 3:7, when connected with the word "way" implies there is a "way" that is not understanding of our wives and unhealthy. So how do I live with my wife in an understanding way? It surely means nothing less than listening. Also required is we understand her well enough to know what an "*understanding way*" is with her. Practically speaking this requires we draw out her dreams, fears, disappointments, and expectations. Make it a goal to know as much about your wife as possible. Understanding my wife requires I have a sensitive spirit. Understanding my wife means out of the work of grace in my heart I call out to that same grace at work in hers. Walking in grace is always healthy. Deep influence invites deeper connection.

I officiated the funeral of a woman some years ago. She left behind a husband and children. At the graveside as I stood next to the husband, I'll never forget these words he said, "I think I gave her everything except myself". I believe he was actually talking to himself, but he stated his thoughts out loud. The tragedy of recognizing too late that he failed to pursue both a connection with and deep influence in any real way grieved him. It will be your tragedy as well if you don't seek to align yourself in an understanding way with your wife and to value her as a partner and sharer of grace.

If you are tempted to think this is no big deal 1 Peter 3:7 ends with these words "…so that your prayers will not be hindered." That will sober you right up. Think of what God is saying there. To neglect seeking to cultivate growing and meaningful connections with our wives will affect our prayers.

A question I have been asked multiple times is something like this, "I have tried but she doesn't respond or care." My answer at those times and now is simply this, God's commands and principles that speak to leading our wives are not conditional upon her response. How our wives may or may not respond doesn't negate the call to lead.

How do we lead our wives in a way that deepens connection and partnership? Let's get to some take-home applications.

Lead your wife with power

Power may seem like an interesting word choice regarding leading our wives. I chose it intentionally due to what brings power into your marriage. What sets your leadership in your marriage apart? It is not authority, age, strength, or position that brings power in our marriages. We need to be aware of the real power that can be present in our marriage relationship. Two avenues of power capture what I believe brings health and vitality into our marriages.

The power of grace and the power of words.

- **The power of grace**

We cannot give what we have not received. You cannot truly express grace if you have not received the grace offered in Christ. It is only by His grace that we can be saved from our sins. Ephesians 2:8 puts it this way, *"For it is by grace you have been saved, through faith—and this is not from yourselves, it is the gift of God—not by works so that no one can boast. (NIV)*

Once again if you have not made a decision to turn to Christ for salvation, please go to the appendix for more specifics on how to come into a relationship with God through Christ. In Christ, we can bring the grace of Christ into our relationship with our spouse.

There are two grace-based words that reveal grace's presence. They are forgiveness and confession. They are easier to write than to express. I am a sinful man and every moment of every day is reliant upon the grace of God. I know that as long as sin resides in me, I need to be rescued from myself. This awareness and my willingness to confess it releases the effects of God's grace. You cannot extend what you have not received. You will not have a deep and lasting influence on your marriage without these two actions being present.

When exercised repentance and forgiveness deepen connection and provide safety. Repentance is confessing your sin and forgiveness is no longer allowing sin to have a hold on your relationship. It is letting go of a hurt or insult that could bring a disconnect in your relationship. To draw out what is in your spouse's heart will require her to feel safe. The presence of confession and the free flow of forgiveness provide this safe place.

Our tendency is to keep score. To overlook the good and zero in on the problems and mistakes of our spouse. Owning our own actions leads us to confession which is crucial if forgiveness is to be present. Starts with you men. If you want to lead your spouse toward health be the first to take a step toward her with an apology or confession without any expectations. Ask for her forgiveness. Do not allow bitterness to take root within your spirit or hers. Hebrews 12:15 warns us, *"See to it that no one falls short of the grace of God and that no bitter root grows up to cause trouble and defile many."*

I think of the word 'defile" in that verse as poison. If you want to poison your marriage or family allow bitterness to sink its tentacles into your heart. For be assured it will "defile" relationships. Counselors and therapists' offices are full of bitter people who are poisoning their relationships because they refuse to forgive.

Leading your marriage means you do not allow bitterness to invade your relationship with your spouse. I have made many mistakes as a husband, but because of the grace of God and my embracing it personally, bitterness has not been allowed access. As one author says, *"Where the grace of God is missed, bitterness is born. But where the grace of God is embraced, forgiveness flourishes. The longer we walk in the garden, the more likely we are to smell like flowers. The more we immerse ourselves in grace, the more likely we are to give grace."*[1]

Husbands take the lead in saying "I am sorry "when you have wronged your wife. Be ready and quick to admit you were wrong and apologize. With no excuses or motives confess your sins and hurtful actions. I call this grace-filled leadership. Be the kind of man your wife looks up to because you live with evident kindness and goodness. Lead her toward health by confessing quickly and forgiving freely.

- **The power of words**

You may notice I have referred to speech in other places in this book. For good reason. Serving from the heart will always involve words in some capacity. It is doubtful you will have much impact without recognition of the power our words have. We have heard and maybe used a phrase like, "It doesn't matter what you say only what you do." It does matter what we say. It matters a lot. It is especially needful in our marriages to flip the power of words for good.

To lead our spouses toward health I encourage you to be intentional with your words. Specifically, phrases like this they need to hear.

"I desire you"
"I love you"
"I cherish you"
"I respect you"
"I missed you"

These and phrases like them bring security and safety into your marriage. Words matter so craft them intentionally. Think ahead of time how to use them. I am working more lately to make my words lighter (apparently, I can be intense) and spicier (flirty is good) with Cyndy. Both expressions bring a positive dynamic along with fanning the flame of romance.

Start by speaking the good into your relationship. We also need to avoid careless words. Your marriage must be a place where true and accurate words are used. Where words are valued and not flippantly spewed around. I am a generalizer with words at times. In my mind, I am trying to communicate a point without the details getting in the way. The danger is that I can be guilty of inaccurate details in my communication. Cyndy cares a great deal about the accuracy of what is said. For her the big picture is important but maybe not as much as the details that paint the picture. Instead, she faces the danger of forgetting the main point of what is being communicated. Neither of our approaches is wrong just different. My approach runs a risk of speaking inaccurate words. She helps me make my words true and accurate.

I told you I would be honest with you in this book, between us, it drives me crazy when she seems to camp on the details. Once again, I see my impatience in this area. I am most definitely a work in progress. To reiterate the point – avoid careless words. Careless words attack emotional and relational health in your spouse's life and in your relationship. Speak words that build up and avoid destructive and careless words. There is one more thing to be said about using words that promote health.

When a relationship fails it usually is not as much what is said, it's because of what is not said. Limited conversation brings limited connection. This means we need to use a proper dosage of words. Take the lead in conversation along with providing your spouse, family, or teams a chance to use words. Rushed dialogue, typed and texted words lose significance not because the words are wrong just that not enough are used.

Texting often results in lazy speech and add-in emojis which can easily deaden the meaning behind words. There is no replacing face-to-face communication of words. When we are not talking, we are not connecting.

As leaders in your marriage foster an atmosphere where the gift of words is freely given. This requires intentionality. Give yourself reminders to speak words that bless. Be a person who in the home and in the marketplace speaks words that build up and encourage. Especially give your spouse a gift of words throughout the day. Especially consider giving her words when she goes to bed. Words she can lay up in her mind and heart as she sleeps.

I am finding in this newer season in my marriage of being "empty nesters" that I need to work harder at engaging in communication. I need to work to speak the right words with the right dosage. It is the right use of words and a proper dosage that will aid you greatly in drawing out your spouse and creating meaningful conversations.

- **The power of prayer**

I must speak to this nonnegotiable if you are going to lead your spouse. Nothing can transform a marriage like calling upon God to grow, protect, and transform our marriages. His power is never in short supply.

I heard about the results of a study on marriages a couple of weeks ago. The one statistic that jumped out at me stated that couples of who prayed for and/or with each other regularly there was a one-percent divorce rate. No that is not a typo. While statistics aren't gospel, they do tell us something. I would like to investigate what those prayers consisted of and the frequency in which they were offered. I am sure these were not flippant and shallow prayers but earnest prayers. It is true it is hard to be angry with and not step toward a spouse when you are praying for them. There is indeed power in prayer.

I believe there is a powerful connection between what 1 Peter 3:7 says about "living with our wives in an understanding way" and praying for them. Because I have sought to know Cyndy as well as I can I know how to pray for her specifically. For example, I pray for her spiritually to grow toward God. I pray for her emotions and name any emotions I know are surfacing within her.

I am grateful for a book I read years ago that gave me insight into how to better pray for Cyndy and recommend it highly to you. It is by Stormie Omartian and is called "The Power of a Praying Husband". She has also written another book called "The Power of a Praying Parent."

I seek to cover Cyndy in prayer when I know she may be walking into an emotionally difficult situation or family dynamic. I pray her mind throughout the day would be bombarded by the Spirit of God. I regularly ask God to give her a growing hunger for God and His Word. After a sent text that pulsates with frustration, I stop to cover her in prayer.

Please understand there are times, albeit seldom thank God, my prayers are through clenched teeth as I battle letting frustration get the best of me. It is hard to remain angry or frustrated and pray for someone at the same time. I believe God is able to do more than I can imagine in the heart, mind, and life of Cyndy. He can transform your spouse's life. God has graciously chosen to respond to our prayers. So, pray!! He will work how and when He wants. He will change our spouses the way He wants. God doesn't care too much how I want Cyndy to change. He has His own agenda for her life. Praying for your spouse is the best way to have a deep and lasting influence in her life.

There are no shortcuts. Praying takes time and concentration. You must prioritize and plan to pray. Do whatever it takes to bathe your spouse in prayer. There is nothing short of God's power available to the man who prays.

Be a defender

I am by nature a protector and defender. I believe all men are in a general sense. Being one who defends their spouse was modeled for me by my dad. No one messed with my mom. If we thought disobeying Dad was bad news, and believe me it was, disobeying Mom brought it to another level.

What does it mean to defend our spouses? Of course, we need to protect our wives from physical harm or danger and ensure their safety. Those who lead well in their marriages provide something more. They provide an atmosphere that is safe. I need to state here that abuse of any kind is evil and an affront to God's design for marriage. Our marriages need to be safe places and those in abusive relationships are anything but safe and need help and need so immediately. There can be no progress relationally until spouses are in a safe environment.

Along with physical protection, as leaders in the home, we are to defend our wives spiritually, emotionally, and relationally.

Spiritually we protect our wives through prayer, worshipping together, and learning about God through the bible together. Husbands you must take the lead in this. It is a direct neglect of your leadership to leave your wife exposed to spiritual attacks, emotional assaults, and relational drift.

To defend your wife, you need to know her. Her vulnerabilities and weaknesses. The mindsets she battles and the level of relational satisfaction. As I mentioned at the beginning of the book leading from the rooftop is invaluable here. Observe and listen. As you learn and observe it will reveal how you can pray for her and encourage her. Leading in the home requires protection. I've already talked about the power in the home of grace, words, and prayer to lead your wife to health.

Leading our wives means we also seek to defend them emotionally. Not because they are weak but because they feel deeply. Some may disagree with me, but I believe there are situations and words that would hurt more than help our wives and we serve them well by deflecting them away. This takes knowing your wife and discerning the moment.

I have wrestled with this point at times throughout our marriage. Because I am a fierce defender of Cyndy I have played the hockey goalie in our marriage. If you can picture a hockey goalie deflecting shot after shot of the puck away from going into the net, you get an idea of the mindset I can get into. While I can be of real help to Cyndy by deflecting negativity from getting to her, I also run the risk of losing out on her needed help and perspective. I also may interfere with how God wants to work in her life. Some of what comes our way may be meant to grow Cyndy but if I am seeking to deflect every puck I can easily get in the way. It takes discernment in this area to protect our wives' thoughts and emotions. I have carried way more than I should have alone because I did not spend the necessary time to pray and think through how to best defend and engage Cyndy.

We also need to defend our wives in relation to the season of marriage. Taking the lead in the ways I have shared already will go a long way in preventing what I call relational rift and drift. Unresolved conflict and relational indifference are lethal and, in my observations, seem to surface when the nest becomes empty. I see a flag when I see parents pressing their children to stay home well into their 20s. While releasing our children is difficult it is a must. Your children should also not be used as a way to avoid difficult adjustments. Husbands you take the lead in that transition and adjustment. Be quick to address arguments and disagreements. Be intentional in seeking to keep connected with your spouse on deepening levels. In doing these things you defend your marriage and make a deep impact possible.

CHAPTER FOUR

Leading Your Children

Dads you must lead with the understanding that if you don't, someone else will.

I want to begin this chapter by letting you know I am sensitive to the fact that some of you grew up in homes that did not have two parents, or you may have had relatives serving as your guardians and the topic of fathers is a tough one for you. In some cases, there may have been an unhealthy relationship with your father that affected your home and the atmosphere where you grew up. Perhaps there was an absence of a father or father figure in your life. Your stories are probably very different than mine. Your stories are a part of who you have become. I am sure your experiences have forged certain mindsets and convictions. The good news is that no matter how hard our younger years were, no matter what you and I may have faced, through God's power and His Word, God can provide for us a new start and a new family legacy. You can begin a new chapter in your family, one of deep influence, which can extend into generations. Now that is an impact, and yes, God can use you to do that! God wants to take you right where you are and grow you to be what your children need.

A few years ago, my mom passed away leaving me and my siblings with no living parents. It has been a difficult adjustment to not having either alive. It remains difficult not to be able to ask for their advice, tell them about our adventures, or see their smile. In a weird way it seemed with mom alive there was still a sense of dad being present.

Mom had a box with Dad's ashes in her room on top of her cabinet. She wanted to be buried with dad so that is where dad's ashes were until she passed. It became a frequent joke that Dad was still hanging around. Through the laughter, I think mentally we had not fully let go. When mom passed it hit hard. When she had just passed and I came to her room my sister Beth was there and we hugged with tears in our eyes she said, "We are orphans now". I joked that she should not write hallmark cards. Yet what she said I knew to be true. In a real way, their voice was gone. I miss their voice speaking into my life. I miss the insights, reactions, and advice they would give about any given topic we'd discuss. I can remember things they said and times together. What I do not have is an orderly accumulation of their experiences and lessons. I wish I had been intentional about recording the many things they spoke about and taught me. The many experiences they learned from. I do not want to make that mistake.

This chapter is about the many things my children have taught me, lessons I have learned, and convictions developed about being the man my kids call dad. I will speak primarily from the perspective of the role of a father; however, parenting is a partnership with the children's mother. As I share some of what I have attempted to do I don't want it to appear I did this by myself. While I have led our home Cyndy has been right at my side.

I remember like yesterday being in the hospital room when my first child was born. Her name is Angela (didn't want to brag and name her angel) so we tried to show humility with who we no doubt knew was our perfect child. I was overwhelmed with the thought I was now to care for Cyndy and now another precious life. Would I be up for it? It didn't take long to realize I was in over my head. Within a week of bringing Angela home, I was carrying her down the steps from upstairs and my socks slipped on the stairs and down I went. The stairway had no real railing and still holding her up in the air and falling I twisted my body able to hold her up setting her on a stair and continued my fall. I popped up quickly and grabbed her before she fell off the stairs. This moment also stands as the greatest athletic feat of my life. Today I ache thinking about it. The message had been sent though this was not going to be as easy as I thought. I had to do this right.

To raise my children drawing from the grace of God required I recognize a few things. My children belong to God before they belong to me. He has entrusted them to me to lead them to a relationship with Jesus Christ and to raise them to live a life for His glory. I am grateful my children have placed their faith in Christ as their Savior. We cannot force our children to trust Jesus, but we must lead them to see their need for Christ as their Savior and teach them He is the only one who can save them.

I can't even begin to express how much I love my children. They bring such craziness, energy, love, and kindness into my life. Each is so different and blesses me in many ways. I have been far from a perfect dad. I have tried very hard though to value my time with them. As has been testified to by so many parents, time still flew by. No matter how I tried to squeeze moments tightly they still passed by. What I have learned, and still am, is that as my children enter different seasons of their lives, they still need Dad. They just need me differently and I still am discovering with each of them how. Every study on parenting can't escape the truth when dads are not actively engaged in their children's lives the children suffer. Whether they are 10 or 20 years old Dad's influence should run deep.

For example, Children with absent fathers are more likely to live in poverty, more likely to end up in prison, more likely to abuse substances, and have friends who abuse substances. Children without fathers are more likely to be obese and struggle academically.[1]

My daughter Angela and I are currently planning to lead a workshop for fathers. The workshop will be a transparent discussion between a dad and his daughter of what every man needs to know to train and shape a complete child. Our goal is to encourage and equip dads with knowledge and hope.

Angela will give voice to the effect a dad has by what he does or fails to do. Even the best-intentioned efforts can cause hurt or leave a child frustrated and worse yet alone. As I prepare for that workshop, I am reflecting on what I sought to be intentional about in shepherding my children's hearts. I also am evaluating what they will need from me in the days ahead.

I had identified five key areas I sought to give special attention to when raising my kids. I have been intentional in my efforts and because my kids are living in a different generation than I grew up I knew my parenting would need to be oriented around God's call to me and who God created them to be. Intentionality was needed if I wanted to be the dad my children needed. I could not wing it if I was to shepherd my children's hearts well. Passivity is not an option. If you don't lead believe me someone else will.

By way of a metaphor, fathers must be in the bridge-building business. To build any bridge requires many pieces of material. We only see the concrete and steel railings but below them are the support structures called piles.

A pile is a vertical support structure that is used, in part, to hold up a bridge. A pile can be made of wood, concrete, or steel. A pile must be sunk deep into the soil beneath the bridge until the end of it reaches the hard sublayer of compacted soil or rock below. The piles together, hammered to a great depth, support the load of the bridge deck. While these piles are not seen they support the bridge deck which makes crossing over possible.

To build (train) a child requires essential "piles". Critical supports that provide a solid road into their future. Intentional supports sunk deep into their hearts and minds. These supports pave the way for your child to walk into adulthood and into a future with purpose, fulfillment, and a sense of identity. Without these supports a child will not be prepared to go into adulthood in a way in which they can flourish. If we neglect these supports we leave them with little confidence or direction.

It is essential each support is based on God's design for the home and their lives. Each support increases in strength when teaching is tied to those truths being modeled. Each support maintains its strength with repetitiveness and intentionality. These supports will make your home a different place than anywhere else. These supports will provide the framework in which you can lead your children at the heart level. There must be intentional teaching, encouragement, and training. What are these supports I am speaking of? They are as follows.

- Love
- Honor
- Protection
- Positive attitude
- Healthy identity

Let me break these supports down.

The Support of Love

I can't imagine any father at seeing their newborn child not thinking I want to love this child. Love is an action word, and it is the action and direction of love that must be fleshed out.

First, it is only God's love that makes any other expressions of love truly possible.

1 John 4:19 says, "We love because He first loved us." The implication is in order for me to truly bring the love required and needed to express to my family I must know God. It is His love flowing out of me that provides what they need from me as a dad. I have often asked myself, "Do the kids see I love God? Do they see the work of Jesus in my life?" I can only hope in the Spirit they have been able to say," Yes".

Secondly, aside from loving God the next best thing I can do for my kids is to love their mother. It is in my observations that many homes are centered on children. Their activities, interests, concerns, plans, and complaints drive the schedule and the priorities in the home. That is not healthy for your home. Your home must be centered on Christ and then on the husband-and-wife relationship. I think I can confidently say my children know I love Cyndy deeply. I think they have seen me sacrifice for her, seek to serve her, and protect her. They have had a front seat to see how far from perfect my efforts have been, but they also have seen the times I have loved well. In my love for Cyndy, they find security as our children. They know Dad isn't going anywhere. To build this support of love starts with loving God and loving your wife.

There are other considerations when addressing what love is and what love does. Perhaps the greatest description of love is found in 1Corinthains 13. Read closely these words.

Love is patient, love is kind. It does not envy, it does not boast, it is not proud. It does not dishonor others, it is not self-seeking, it is not easily angered, it keeps no record of wrongs. Love does not delight in evil but rejoices with the truth. It always protects, always trusts, always hopes, always perseveres. 1Corinthians 13:4-7 (NIV)

God would not have given us a description of His love in action if we did not need it. In our selfish inclinations and distortions of love God wanted to make it clear to us. The list reads nice and looks good on a plaque but living these descriptors of love is not so easy.

Above all love is action and as you look at 1 Corinthians 13 the actions of love are exacting and ongoing. To build the support of love will require you to think through what it would look like in the lives of your children.

- **Love is presence**

Love is being present in such a way that you can express patience, kindness etc. You simply cannot express love at a distance. It requires engagement. While I am convicted about the ways I have not measured up to God's description of love in 1 Corinthians 13, I also find it incredibly helpful for me in evaluating and pursuing this kind of love. Whether your children are five or like mine in their mid-20s love is being present and always will be.

When Angela, my oldest child, was little she was helping me lay block on an addition to our house. She was always my little helper and could name and use construction tools quite well. I take great joy knowing I can ask my daughter to hand me a speed square, crescent wrench, level, or most any tool and she will get me each one.

On this particular day, as we were finishing our project up, she asked what her reward would be for helping me. I asked her what she'd like, and she said, "I want to play Barbie Uno with you". I tear up sharing that story. I think I remember it so well because of how precious that moment was and how important my presence was in her life. Many board games, road trips, athletic events, horse shows, and so many other activities were a high priority on my calendar. I knew I had to be there. My presence communicated my love and support. My youngest Emily when she played basketball would be in the game and searching for me as she ran down the court. Not what a coach wants to see but this daddy loved it! Even more, I knew she wanted me there. A child can only hear so many excuses about not showing up at their events. After a while, your words will mean very little. Love is presence. The regrets I carry as a father almost always revolve around not being truly present with my children. Both when physically absent and mentally absent. Both are harmful and unloving.

- **Love is affection**

Because love is expressive, affection must be regularly given in doses. C.S. Lewis once said, "Affection is responsible for nine-tenths of whatever solid and durable happiness there is in our lives."

I was intentional in giving hugs, kisses, and holding their hands when we took walks. I learned in those moments that my kids held my hands and hugged me because it made them feel safe. I held their hands and hugged them because it made me feel whole. I truly treasure every hug and kiss I get. I believe hugs are a great way to express our love. They are more significant than we realize. Years ago, I wrote down something in my journal that I saw posted on the wall at Milwaukee Children's Hospital. It stated that touch is very important for development and bonding. It said studies have shown that positive touch can:

- Slow heart rate
- Lower blood pressure
- Help regulate breathing
- Improve weight gain
- Lower stress hormones
- Decrease pain levels
- Facilitate bonding

With just those benefits alone, why would we not hug and give a positive touch to others, especially our children? Hug your family often. I am a hugger, and I am proud of it. According to author Paul Planet, I am a health nut. He writes:

Hugging is very healthy. It helps the body's immune system. It keeps you healthier. It cures depression and reduces stress. It induces sleep. It is invigorating. It is rejuvenating. It has no unpleasant side effects. Hugging is nothing less than a miracle drug. Hugging is all-natural. It is organic and naturally sweet. It contains no pesticides, preservatives, or artificial ingredients, and it is 100% wholesome.

Hugging is practically perfect. There are no movable parts and no batteries to wear out, no periodic check-ups, no monthly payments, and no insurance requirements. It offers no energy consumption and returns a high-energy yield while being inflation-proof, nonfattening, theft-proof, non-taxable, nonpolluting, and fully returnable.[2]

Love is affection. If fathers don't show affection there is a chance your child will seek it in unhealthy ways and with ungodly persons. I can hear some of you now, "Well I don't show affection because I'm not that kind of person." Affection is a choice so simply make the choice. We are all wired to show and receive affection. Love makes the choice to show affection.

Affection connects at the heart level and when married to the other expressions of love bring deep connection. Now go hug your child. I'll wait.

- **Love is truth-telling**

There can be no deep influence in your child's life if you cannot speak the truth. There is little truth spoken at the shallow level. The initial years of a child's life lay the groundwork for trust and security.

A caring, affectionate, and involved father contributes significantly to a child's emotional development, fostering safety and confidence that forms the bedrock of their relationship. The bedrock of love and trust allows for dads to be able to speak truth into their child's life.

Speaking truth to our children can have a sharp edge to it. It is hard to speak and hard to receive the truth but is needed for growth. My children haven't liked the times, and still don't, when I speak hard truth to them, but they know I love them. My presence and affection have been a part of their whole lives and they know I love them enough to tell them the truth. In my mind, it is unloving to withhold what could help protect and help children grow.

Just like we cannot withhold truth because it is difficult to speak we also cannot withhold discipline. Disciplining our children falls under loving them as discipline and love are never separated in God's design. I believe in appropriate corporal discipline. I know it's almost culturally taboo, but I don't care to take cues from the culture. Children grow up more responsible and respectful. They need to be taught early in their life that there are consequences.

As fathers called to lead young children, we need to explain the unacceptable behavior and at times spank them. I had a plan when I disciplined my children. I believe it is a must after the act of discipline to end with a hug, and I liked to pray over them when they were younger. I wanted them to connect discipline with love and the help God gives for obedience.

Whether younger or teenage years children should not be surprised they were disciplined. If they are surprised, you need to clarify again the boundaries and behaviors. Fathers help them to understand they were spanked as a result of their disobedience and because of love. We are seeing increasing amounts of disrespect in our culture, and I know it sounds simplistic, but a little spank on the backside and soap in the mouth would help with that. These times also provide valuable teaching moments to communicate we are all under God's authority and must submit to Him or there are consequences. Truth-telling and discipline are expressions of love that reveal to dads and kids alike the need for grace.

Fathers serve as role models for their children, shaping their beliefs, behaviors, and perceptions. A loving, honest father figure instills confidence, encourages ambition, and helps foster independence in his son's and daughter's life choices. He wraps his actions in love and grace. In doing so he builds a support for a flourishing future.

The Support of Honor

Honor has many uses, all of them good. At the core is value. If you are called a man a *man of honor*, you are respected. If someone *honors* you, they recognize and award you for your achievements. The term *honor* has always been a word used to describe men and women of high moral worth or great achievement. It can be used as either a noun or verb, and in many different settings. People graduate from college with honors, meaning they have outstanding academic achievements. A woman of honor is pure and decent. Soldiers are buried with full military honors, which means they are given gun salutes and trumpet calls and the nation's fullest respect. Value is expressed when we show honor.

Building the support of honor requires us to consider what showing value to children looks like. Honoring our children includes acts like listening to their heart's cries, and celebrating their God-given personalities, successes, and differences.

There have been trips and conferences I have attended over the years in which I have picked up a gift or trinket for Cyndy or the kids. At times they would be fragile, and I would need to wrap them in something to prevent them from being damaged so they could be appreciated. I wrapped them and was careful with the gift because it had value. Because we treat carefully what we value. Likewise, we treat carefully who we honor. Show your children how much you value them by treating them carefully. This requires you to appreciate their differences and not to compare them with others. Your kids will, and it doesn't change when they are in their 20s, compare how they felt they were treated compared to their siblings and their friends. I am not talking about being unfair but affirming each other's differences and responding to each of them in a way that shows you value them. Leading your children well in this area also includes helping them process their unique designs and gifts and what that could look like as they live out of these.

For example, my daughter Emily has a unique way of speaking that can sell ideas and plans. She is both creative and relentless in this. While this frustrated my wife and I when she would craft a defense of why she should do things we grew to admire her persistence. My wife and I over the years spoke of this and considered where Emily should pursue working. We never envisioned how this is playing out now in her adult years as an adult home care supervisor. She is a strong advocate for the challenged adults she oversees. Her relentlessness and creativity have allowed her to come up with ways to help others. Whether to "higher ups", the police, or other concerned persons she unapologetically stands with those she cares for and seeks solutions not simply to complain and demean. It is fun to see how her God-given design is on display. I want to recognize, affirm, and honor her in this. I know I will not have a deep and lasting influence without showing honor.

I value words. Someone who gets me a card or takes the time to write me a note communicates to me value. Your child may feel valued more with another expression. If you are not sure ask them what makes them feel most loved and valued. You honor your children by showing them they are more valuable than anything else you could have on your calendar.

As I periodically read through some of my journals, I am struck by how many simple entries there are about what may seem like insignificant moments. Here are some of the entries:

"I had a really nice time with Angela at a home school BB (basketball) game, Thank you Lord for good times with my Angela"

"I was home last night with the family, and we had a blast being together."

"I enjoyed playing games with Ben today."

"I enjoy watching my kids participate in sports."

"We had fun at the waterpark today."

"I enjoyed watching David play football tonight".

"Emily did great at the horse show today"

Not any one of the moments is monumental, but they add up to communicating much value. I have and always will believe it's the sum total of being present in the moments that add up to a powerful impact in the long run. Dads your children are looking for you at their activities. Don't for a moment think they are unaware of your presence. Show them honor by your presence! (Remember love is presence)

We celebrate what we value! Make birthdays and accomplishments a big deal. Show them you are their biggest fan. Cyndy helped me do this as she is very creative in ways to celebrate.

Some of the greatest moments in my life were when I was blessed to baptize all four of my children. All at different times and each a powerful moment. To see your children choose to trust Jesus Christ as their Lord and Savior is as good as it gets. To be present and a part of their public proclamation of their faith is a real reason to celebrate. In celebrating them you celebrate the grace of God!

Honor your children by celebrating them. For if we honor them, and truly communicate their value, we'll give them the freedom to continue to make good choices based on their own character.

The Support of Protection

Dads you play the role of protector in your home; at least you better. This role of protector has been ridiculed and even attacked by post-modernists and their allies in the media. Unfortunately, many fathers have given culture's voice authority over the role they play in their children's lives. To those who ascribe to the outdated traditional role of a father as a protector, I can only say "you are a fool" and totally unaware of the needs of children.

The areas we must give special attention to are physical, spiritual, emotional, and relational protection. The idea of *physical protection* is easiest for us as dads. However, the dangers come from different directions as they grow. When my children were little, I didn't have to be concerned about online stalkers and predators. Add to the increase in sex trafficking and online dating we must be ever-vigilant. When meeting men my daughters may be dating, I seek to be honest and direct and make sure I project a physical barrier they will encounter should they mess with my daughter. While my one son hasn't ever dated, my other son has, and with his girlfriends, I have tried to project a father figure that would make them feel safe.

A dad must shield his family from the outside world that seeks to seduce them toward dangerous and often disgusting activities and pursuits. It is crucial we teach them how to cope with these before they walk across that bridge to their future. Our children cannot thrive in an atmosphere where they feel vulnerable, threatened, and anxious. Dads are the ones members of the family come to when they feel anxious, confused, or threatened. This was true when I grew up and when my children were in the home. If anyone talked down to my children, I would defend their honor and make clear in no uncertain terms how valuable my children are. Mom's arms bring children comfort Dad's arms bring safety and security.

I knew what protection looked like when my children were small, but what does it look like now that they're grown up? What will it look like when they get married? This being a dad stuff takes sustained commitment. This is especially true in the area of providing *spiritual protection*. I'd like to highlight the primary ways we can protect our children.

- **Protection through teaching**

You simply cannot have a deep influence on your children's life if you do not teach them. There are a multitude of voices calling out for your children's attention and to be honest most are deceptive in our culture. They must hear your voice above the others. You protect them when your voice echoes what God's voice says through Scripture.

However, it is not teaching from a lofty perch but teaching as one under the same authority as our children. We as parents are in need of God's gracious Word as much as our children. Communicating this to them is helpful for both your children and yourself.

God's Word is replete with instructions for parents to teach their children what truly matters. He calls us to exercise and teach values such as wisdom, understanding, and discipline. We are to hold truths and values out to our children for them to grab ahold of and carry into their world and future. Dad, you have a responsibility to help your children slip past the imperceptible but distorted values they are being exposed to so over time they can innately respond with God-given values.

Values are vital and this is especially seen in the reality everyone holds to values. I see three possible foundations for our beliefs and the values we hold.

1. Self-determines what is true and right.
2. Society determines what is true and right.
3. The Sovereign Lord determines what is true and right.

With this understanding, our children are more than likely hearing distortions from two of the three sources I mentioned above. This tells me as a dad I better be teaching and repeating often what God sees as right and of value. If your children are grown and out of the home this does not stop. You still are responsible for teaching them until they establish their own homes.

We begin with the truth the fundamental values of life are to be found in the character of God that existed before the world was made. We must pass on a well-rounded picture of who God is. God is holy, good, just, and righteous. God always acts in ways that are true to His character.

We are told the "fear of the Lord is the beginning of wisdom". Proverbs 1:7(NIV). Teaching about God and His character sets our children's learning on the path of wisdom. God's laws and commandments require obedience or there are consequences for God's character demands it.

A former president was interviewed about some of the choices he made in his presidency and personal life, and he said something along the lines of "morals evolve over time". It was hard to hear this from a leader in our nation. This is a lie. God's values (morals) do not evolve because God does not evolve. He is and always has been perfect. Dads must adopt and teach the values of a perfect God. If we do not teach His values, we leave our children at the mercy of the distortions that bombard them. The values of society and often the self are unfulfilling and destructive.

Wisdom was considered by the ancients as a system of values handed down to us by God. This wisdom enabled them to live and be governed by the Sovereign Lord's standards and not by self-determined or societal values/standards. I believe God wants us to value wisdom for from it flows skillful living that aligns with moral standards that produce lasting value for God and the community we live.

The Bible uses other words connected with wisdom. Words such as understanding, discipline, insight, prudence, right, just, fair. Each of these words speaks toward a value system. We are to value wisdom, understanding, and discipline.

There are several passages from the Book of Proverbs that show the connection between wisdom, understanding, and discipline. These three make an important part of the curriculum we need to teach children. Wisdom, understanding, and discipline will protect our children.

Proverbs 1 makes the connection between the communication of the fear of the Lord (Wisdom) and the responsibility of the Father. The teaching from the father is to be intentional as evidenced by the sheer volume of verses that address a "son" from a father. Here is a sampling.

2:1 "My Son, if you will receive my teachings…."

3:1 "My Son, do not forget my teaching…."

3:11 "My Son, do not reject Lord's discipline…"

3:21 "My Son, let them (wisdom & understanding) not depart from your sight."

4:1-2 "Hear, O Sons …… I give you sound teaching, do not abandon my instruction."

4:10 "Hear, my son, and accept my sayings."

4:20 "My Son, give attention to my words."

5:1 "My Son, give attention to my wisdom."

6:1 "My Son, if you…."

7:1 "My Son, keep my words. And treasure my commandments within you."

8:32 "Now, therefore, O Sons, listen to me, for blessed are they who keep my ways."

There is no mistaking the direction the teaching takes and who is responsible. I grieve when I read the studies that show that moms have to lead spiritually in their homes because fathers are not engaged in any Bible teaching, or in leading the family to church, or even not attending themselves. We have a large population of young men adrift because they had no fathers to steer them toward God. Dads you cannot abdicate your call and leave your children's mother having to take the reins.

Teaching from a father brings a solid and at times sober vibe. There is a soundness and rightness that exudes from the above Proverbs passages. The teaching of a father is serious and should carry a sense of "dad means business". They know you mean business because of the priority you place on teaching and training. Give attention to what you need to teach and ways you will do that. Start small. Even with the best intentions none of us will cover everything our children should know but we do need to prioritize what is most important and be intentional in conveying that. We keep repeating that which is at the top of our list. Repetition communicates priority. Whether in the home or workplace we repeat what matters most.

I have a deep appreciation for family and friends. The value was instilled in me as a youngster, and I observed the benefits over and over of investing in relationships with family and friends. I am very close to my siblings, and I know my children notice that and are drawn to that. We communicate appreciation for each other and are affectionate toward each other. We are most certainly known for our laughter and love. I have deep and rich friendships my children observe. Along with observation my children heard from me how important family and friends are.

Now in their 20's they reach out to and meet up with one another regularly. They have consistently chosen and invested in good friendships. These choices are not accidental. Growing up I repeated the significance of friendships and helping and watching over each other as siblings. Today I love to hear them talk about spending time together, texting each other, and helping each other. I love how my son David who is now serving with the Navy calls his siblings to stay in touch. They are still learning what I taught them.

Passive parenting is like passive farming. Without diligent cultivation, we can expect little more than a harvest of weeds. It is very unloving and negligent to forsake teaching and values and neglect the discipline of your children. Your teaching of God's values will protect them throughout their life. Schools, clubs, and youth groups can be very good avenues for children to learn good values, but they will never replace the importance and priority of a father's teaching. I just recently came across Proverbs 14:26 which makes the connection of the transaction of a father to a child.

Whoever fears the Lord has a secure fortress, and for their children it will be a refuge. Proverbs 14:26 (NIV)

See it? Fearing God brings security, and specifically for children. Who will children learn the fear of the Lord from? Fathers! I take great delight in hearing my children say something like, "I know what you would say Dad." about a variety of things. It means I have been consistent in teaching them.

If you want to protect your children from the harmful deception of the culture and Satan's lies live out and teach God's truth.

- **Protection through prayer**

When leafing through one of my journals recently I came across this entry, *"Angela passed her driver's test today. I am very excited for her. She was really nervous and recognized how big of a moment this is and that I get to share it with her is fun. I thank you, God for allowing me to experience this moment. Please keep her safe as she drives and please protect her from the enemy who would seek to destroy her and the lives of all the kids."*

In the joy of the moment, God used my prayer to bring an intense moment of prayer of spiritual protection. Our children need those protecting prayers through all seasons of life. My prayers for my children often are protecting prayers. These prayers were very different when they were in grade school, and then middle school, high school, and now when they are grown and out of the house. What they are exposed to and at what maturity level they are requires us to know how to best help them.

The Bible says that there is a spiritual battle taking place in the unseen realm. This is an ongoing battle in which the demonic realm seeks to harm our children. The author of the book of Ephesians puts it this way,

For our struggle is not against flesh and blood, but against the rulers, against the authorities, against the powers of this dark world and against the spiritual forces of evil in the heavenly realms. (Ephesians 6:12 NIV)

The attacks will continue to come, and I will never stop protecting them by covering them in prayer and seeking to walk in obedience to my Savior Jesus. You leave your children vulnerable to these attacks when you personally walk in rebellion against God and do not pray for them and over them.

One o'clock in the afternoon and nine o'clock at night are two important times in my day. Being completely convinced of my responsibility to protect my children in prayer I began a discipline a couple of years back. Along with prayer time during my morning devotions, at one o'clock my phone gives me a reminder to pray for my sons Benjamin and David. I stop what I am doing and spend a moment in prayer for them. At nine o'clock at night, I get a reminder to pray for my daughters Angela and Emily. At least twice each day I devote time to covering my children with prayer. God will also lay them on my heart at other times, but I don't want to drop the ball in protecting my children.

I encourage you to intentionally carve out time to cover your children in prayer. Make it a point to ask how they need prayer periodically. I give you little hope of having a deep and lasting influence in your children's lives without praying for and over them.

- **Protection through emotional sensitivity**

Another area where protection is needed is *our children's emotions.* Dads we must work on this one. I have found this true even more so the older they get. Especially in the lives of my daughters. A positive and supportive father figure instills emotional balance, and confidence, encourages ambition, and helps foster independence in his children's life choices.

The father–child relationship is fertile ground for learning emotional intelligence. Healthy communication and expression of feelings within this bond enable children to navigate relationships, develop empathy, and handle emotions effectively.

Dads seek to maintain open and honest dialogue. Encouraging open communication fosters trust and understanding. Fathers who actively engage in conversations with their children create a safe space for expressing thoughts, feelings, and concerns.

I know often I would try to do this, and the kids didn't really seem interested. But I know the effort lets them know the door is open to have honest personal discussions. So don't be discouraged when you try and there seems little to no engagement. This is especially true with my sons. I am committed to remaining open and honest in my communication with them and every now and then they engage. I compare it to a football running back. When you have a great running back you keep giving him the ball because sooner or later, he is going to break off a long run. But you got to give the running back touches.

Leading Those You Love

With your children keep giving them opportunities (touches) to open up and sooner or later one discussion will open up and you will give them what they need, a safe place to share and process.

Dads learn to listen and show empathy. Actively listening and showing empathy towards a child's emotions validate their experiences, strengthening the emotional bond between you and your child. Let's be honest, emotions can be explosive at certain points in your children's lives. At times they might not even understand them. My one child is in their mid-20's said to me a couple of months ago, "I am sorry I don't know why I am so emotional." That was not the first time that had occurred, nor will it be the last.

Another way we can protect our child's emotions by proactively engaging in such a way we deepen connections with them. Engaging in shared activities, hobbies, or adventures nurtures a bond built on shared experiences, creating cherished memories and reinforcing the connection. A supportive and involved father figure instills confidence and assertiveness in children, helping them navigate challenges with resilience.

My son Benjamin has had to face several heart surgeries beginning five days after his birth. He has had several more throughout his childhood. We were sensitive to his emotions of fear and sadness during these times. We worked to help him express those emotions without minimizing them. He has shown great determination each time in the recovery process. He is what I call a gamer. Whether I realized it or not some of his approach and resilience I believe were positively affected by our emotional sensitivity to him during his challenges.

While Angela needs to take her foot off the gas in regard to activities, Emily is ambitious in wanting to accomplish much in life. She would say she is not a fan of academic pursuits but does want to excel in areas she is engaged in.

After considering physical, spiritual, and emotional protection we must work hard to protect our relationships with our children. This *relational protection* requires emotional connection and sensitivity. Protecting a relationship is done through acts of forgiveness, restoration, and release. It is also done in teaching the same to your kids.

I can honestly say one of the things I have done over the years is apologize when I wronged one of my children. I have gotten angry and yelled, missed a moment when they needed me, or minimized their inner world or interests. Yet when I recognized it, I sought to say "I am sorry". As you know those are hard words to say to our kids.

If we value our relationships, we must own up to how we have hurt them and not allow the hurt to fester. I have had numerous conversations with people in counseling over the years who were facing challenges and to one degree or another were rooted in their broken relationship with their dad. Neither would seek forgiveness. If you want to protect your children then take the first step in seeking forgiveness. Forgiveness is a huge step toward restoration, but it is not the only step. Forgiveness is a choice and don't let anyone tell you it is a process. Either you forgive or you don't. Forgiveness does not mean you forget but that you no longer hold the wrong done to you over their head.

Restoration can be a process. Especially if the wrong was one that violated boundaries. In these cases, appropriate boundaries need to be set to enable the restoration to continue. God can restore even the most messed up of family dynamics. But it won't happen without humility and seeking and extending forgiveness.

Finally, somewhere in the process, there needs to be a release. A release of the wrong and its infringement on your relationships. Wrongs remembered and brought up again and again are unhealthy and to be honest, are immature. Dads provide relational protection by modeling and teaching forgiveness, restoration, and release.

Here is where I find the challenge in regard to protecting my children. I do not want any hardships to come to them. Nor do you, I am sure. However, God uses difficult times to grow our children and to cooperate with God's agenda in my children's life is not easy. My children are all at different places in their maturity and growth. They all had, have, and will face difficulties. Ones I wish they wouldn't have to. Yet the grace of God that loves me too much to let me stay the way I am is also the grace of God I need to extend to not shield them from the work of God in their life.

It is hard to watch your children face consequences and hard not to gloss over their poor choices as if they are simply having a bad day. If I spare my children from the suffering and consequences of their behavior, I will also be sparing them from the shaping. My children are not the work of my hands but the work of God's hands. So don't shield your child from the consequences of sinful and poor behavior. Allow them to discover the grace that will free and shape them just as it has and is you.

The Support of a Positive attitude

Another key support we need to build into our children's lives so they can grow with stability and confidence is one of a healthy and hope-filled attitude. Anyone who knows me would say how much I value a positive attitude. Nothing good has ever come from negativity. Even criticism, if it produces anything good, must come packaged in the hope of positive change. I speak often in this book on the value of a positive attitude because of its significance. I have always desired to be a purveyor of hope in my family's lives. No situation is beyond the ability of God to transform it. This I believe in every fiber of my being. I have seen and experienced the miraculous hand of God.

When it comes to preparing the way for your children into their future the support of a positive attitude bears fruit for the immediate and the future. The value of a positive attitude is seen in numerous studies. Studies show that one who can live with this type of attitude experiences many positive benefits. They prove to be a good friend, school and work success is enhanced, achievement and enjoyment of sports are increased, and they possess hope for the future. One particular benefit that jumps out is those who live with a positive attitude show strong mental health. We are told there is a quickly ascending mental health problem today and is especially prevalent in this young generation. Which our youth director tells me is called the Alpha generation. It is not hard to stand back and see the volatility, divisiveness, and negativity all around us. We should not be surprised this atmosphere has created defeat, discouragement, and hopelessness throughout all generations. Dads in light of this, your home must be a different place. A much different place where within your walls there is great positivity.

How do we create a positive atmosphere in our homes where our children regularly operate from a positive posture?

- **Start with gratitude**.

Remind your children how blessed they are. Periodically ask them what they are grateful for. At times around the table, we'd ask what was your favorite part of the day. It was an intentional question asked to move the kids from camping on any negative incidents that may have occurred. When November rolled around my wife made a large Thanksgiving tree that was bare at the beginning of the month. Each day we each would write on a leaf one thing we were thankful for. And hang it on the tree. When we got to the last third of the month it forced us all to really evaluate how deep our blessings run. Gratefulness and negativity are not traveling partners.

Why not initiate regular family times to identify blessings in your life? When my children were young, and I was tucking them I often asked them what made them happy that day. I wanted them to see the presence of blessings and positivity even if the day included some hard stuff. Choose gratefulness and lead your children in that direction and watch as discussions and attitudes become more positive. This atmosphere allows kids to make mistakes and learn from them. Of course, the other supports I've spoken of when interlocked with this one give greater strength.

- **Identify opportunities**

In the midst of our day-to-day circumstances, God is always at work. Knowing that provides a different perspective. A positive one. We can learn to see God's hand at work. This brings not only an expectancy to each encounter and situation but also energy to live positively.

I truly hope and pray that my children can pick up the mantle from my life, embrace any successes, and not allow any of my imperfections and failures to restrict their growth. I want to fuel their determination to do better. I want them to learn to see opportunities to serve rather than the negativity that may be on the surface. I hope they learn from me life is not determined so much by failures or successes as by our perspective on these failures and successes. It is my belief there is no one better to teach them than Dad.

Job losses, financial pressures, health issues, and failed plans all have great potential to teach our children to identify opportunities for good rather than simply negative experiences.

Leadership in the home has to do with both protection and direction. Directing your children to opportunities to serve and grow. I have encouraged all my children to serve on a short-term mission trip. My two daughters both did so in Guatemala. This opportunity allowed them the opportunity to serve the needs of others, see a different reality, and recognize their blessings.

- **Laugh together**

Take every opportunity to laugh and bring joy to your children and those you lead, love, and serve. It is truly life-giving. Being lighthearted in a serious world is one way to serve your children. Laughter is the best medicine for the tension, worries, and challenges our children face. Learn to laugh at yourself and look for a moment to help your children smile or laugh.

I keep coming back to the word intentional. Fathers make a plan to include among other things building a positive attitude.

The Support of a Healthy Identity

As I evaluate how I have raised my children this is the one area I was unaware of the deeper of significance. I underestimated the pressure the culture has placed on this generation and how that would affect their struggle with identity. In my mind, I am a child of God before I am anything else. Clear and simple in my mind. That is who I am in God's eyes. Yet it took me some time to get to living from this conviction. But in my children's lives, especially my daughters, there are so many cultural voices screaming for them to attach their identity to any number of things. Dads you play a significant role in helping your children gain a sense of a true God-given identity.

In God's perfect plan, men and women and their children were meant to get their foundational identity vertically. From the beginning of creation the identity He gave would guide His creation in how they viewed themselves, their community, and their vocation. It would underscore their purpose and give meaning to their pursuits. This identity from above was to provide daily guidance along with setting hedges around their minds and hearts. Since the fall of the very first man and woman, people have looked horizontally for what they were designed to look for above. Your children are being tempted to look at people, places, and things to do for them what only a healthy identity can do for them. By healthy identity, I mean an identity rooted in God.

I came across this study about dads and daughters that affirms this. The study found that daughters who believe that their fathers care about them have significantly fewer suicide attempts and fewer instances of body dissatisfaction, depression, low self-esteem, substance abuse, and unhealthy weight.[3]

Dads, do you see that? This is no small thing. To help foster, develop, and support the healthy identity of your children will require an awareness of cultural lies and strategies. My wife has taken the girls clothes shopping over the years and as the years progressed, she has returned telling me how hard it was to find any clothes that are remotely modest. Make no mistake, that is a strategy of a culture over-sexualized. Now any new fashion on tik-toc, Instagram, and promoted by influencers are going to be what the stores sell. Don't cave in. Don't compromise. If you do you will hinder your children from the development of a healthy self-esteem and identity. Praise, affirm, and remind your children often how God and you feel about them.

A healthy and whole identity is rooted in knowing God and is revealed in the truths of the Bible. God wants those who trust in Jesus Christ as their Savior to know who they truly are. God wants you personally to know your true identity. At the core of this healthy identity is the truth as a believer in Jesus Christ you are accepted and secure in Christ. A healthy identity is rooted in grace. As God's grace is working in my heart and mind I see myself in light of what Jesus has done for me and who He sees me as.

Consider these verses which speak to one's identity as a Christian. I strongly recommend reading and discussing them with your children.

John 1:12	You are God's child
John 15:15	You are Christ's friend
Romans 5:1	You have been justified
1 Corinthians 6:20	You have been bought with a price, you belong to God
1 Corinthians 12:27	You are a member of the body of Christ
Ephesians 1:5	You have been adopted as God's child

Ephesians 2:18	You have direct access to God through the Holy Spirit
Colossians 1:14	You have been redeemed and forgiven of all your sins
Colossians 2:10	You are complete in Christ
Romans 8:1-2	You are free forever from condemnation
Romans 8:28	You are assured that all things work together for good
Romans 8:33-34	You are justified and free from any condemning charges against you
Romans 8:35	You cannot be separated from the love of God in Christ Jesus
Colossians 3:3	You are hidden with Christ in God
Philippians 3:20	You are a citizen of Heaven
Hebrews 4:16	You can draw near to His throne and receive grace and mercy
1 John 5:1, 4	You are born of God, and you have overcome the world
1 John 5:18	You are born of God and the evil one cannot touch you
John 15:16	You have been chosen and appointed to bear fruit
Acts 1:8	You have received power, you are a personal witness of Christ's
1 Corinthians 3:16	You are God's temple
2 Corinthians 5:17-18	You are a new creation, a minister of reconciliation
2 Corinthians 5:20	You are an ambassador for Christ
2 Corinthians 6:1	You are God's coworker
Ephesians 2:6	You are seated with Christ in the heavenly realm
Ephesians 2:10	You are God's workmanship
Ephesians 3:12	You may approach God with freedom and confidence

Philippians 4:13   You can do all things through Christ who strengthens you

As I read all these, It is clear God is serious about us knowing who we are in Him. All these verses, and there are many more, reveal that having an identity rooted in Christ is the defining element of how a person makes sense of who he/she is and what they are supposed to be doing. Any distorted identity will leave divided minds and unsettled hearts in our children.

Distorted identities will eventually lead to idolatry as one seeks to get from creation what can only come from their creator.

Stand personally in the promises above and help your children stand in them. When leaders forget that in Christ, they are God's child above all else, the role of being a dad becomes blurred. Dads remind yourself often who you are in Christ. You are a child of God before you are any of the roles you carry out. Having a healthy identity leads to being a healthy leader.

Certainly, our children need to be taught and reminded throughout their lives of who they are in Christ. They are not their occupations. They are not their achievements. Those do not form their identities. God does.

In the season of life my children are in the issue of identity seems so much greater. I am having to think harder about how to speak into their lives the truth about who they really are. Flowing out of a healthy identity is character. Trace the character of a person and you will get an idea of how they view themselves. Identity and character travel together. Low self-worth often results in careless behaviors. Identity rooted in self and culture can lead only to rebellion.

What character traits I see as of great worth such as integrity, purity, truth-telling, and kindness are valued lightly.

As I write this, we are weeks away from the 2024 elections. Watching the debates and commercials I am struck by the lack of integrity, kindness, and absence of honesty along both aisles. Even from the highest office in our land, there is a message to our children Godly qualities are optional "if you want to get ahead." That cannot be the message in our homes. You are to lead your family to be a different home. Different from the culture. Building your child's identity based on God's Word is a team effort with your spouse. However, dads you take the lead!

I recognized I was responsible for, as best I could, lead our home and its values and behaviors to be a place that was different. A home where the kids' friends would come and find the atmosphere inviting and safe from the world's pressures.

Dads, releasing your child into an unknown future is difficult but you must release them. When you build these supports you build a bridge where your child can go into their future confident, assured, armed with a healthy sense of identity, and successful in what matters. I have confidence and assurance as I pursue building these supports that my efforts will bear fruit.

The Bible speaks to the need for and the promise that accompanies the training of our children.

*Start **child**ren off on the way they should go, and even when they are old, they will not turn from it. Proverbs 22:6 (NIV)*

*Fathers do not exasperate your **child**ren; instead, bring them up in the training and instruction of the Lord Ephesians 6:4 (NIV)*

A father's impact on the lives of his children continues to stand out in study after study. Consider these words I came across:

"When only mom takes her sons to church while they're growing up, approximately 15 percent of boys remain churchgoers after they become adults. However, if dad takes an active role with mom in leading the family to church, the number who continue their spiritual journey increases to somewhere around 75 percent. That's a significant difference that speaks to the power men have to be spiritual influences on their sons."[4]

Rick Johnson – Better Dads, Stronger Dads

Lead in getting your family to a solid Bible Church. Lead by never stopping moving your education forward. Be a dad whose kids say, "Dad never stops learning. He is always trying to get better. Dad pursues greater impact and influence. Dads keep building these supports throughout the season of your children's lives. They are depending on you.

Having said that it bears pointing out again that Dads need to work in partnership with their wife or children's mom. Don't be an island. Don't make the mistake of always assuming unilateral authority or that she is on the same page. Your leadership is necessary to find agreement on your decisions, plans, discipline, and other parenting efforts. As with other leadership contexts building a "we" mindset bears the most fruit. Take a team approach in leading the home.

Today my children struggle at times, as did I at their age, but I believe intentionality in my efforts will bear fruit. I will not be an absent or uninvolved dad. I will, until my dying breath, seek to love and serve and provide the needed support I have shared. I don't know everything for sure. What I do know is that my children need a dad who will build supports on a solid foundation of grace that will provide a bridge into the future God has for them.

CHAPTER FIVE

Leading Your Teams

What team am I talking about? Your team! When I use the word "teams" I am referring to any group you may lead. It could be a department you lead at your place of employment. It perhaps is an organization you belong to. It might be a school sports team or any other group you are responsible for leading in some capacity. These serve as your teams.

Leadership in these groups is a privilege and an opportunity to help people to develop and grow. I have learned people often don't consider how to grow others in these contexts. I believe these God-given opportunities are fertile ground for personally having a positive impact.

There are three types of people

- Those who are moveable
- Those who are immovable
- Those who move them

Leaders move others. Whether it be their spouse, child, co-workers, or players. They move others toward being their best. This is especially true when we consider the various groups we may lead. This does not happen by accident. Passivity in leadership grows no one. I hope to convince and equip you to move from position-based leadership to one of personal impact. I want to give you some encouragement which you can apply in leading your team(s).

Be available

As the leader, you need to spend a lot of time with your team or staff in order to multiply yourself. This investment shows your commitment to them as a person first and as a co-worker second. It is a big step in eliminating a power structure that produces self-preservation and fear. This requires humility. It is hard to work in an atmosphere when you are looking over your shoulder for the shoe to drop. It is hard to operate in an environment where you feel alone and unwanted or unneeded.

I read a report recently about church staff and the escalating number who feel isolated and overwhelmed. I am sure that part of what is feeding their feelings is lack of personal engagement with those leading them. When you work, play, and serve with a leader who demonstrates they are there for you it reduces much stress. An open door, a flexible schedule, and a listening ear are the signs of approachability. You are wise to keep each.

Many years ago, I began a practice of meeting with my staff in their office, not mine. I wanted to somehow show I valued and esteemed them by not expecting them to come to me, but I wanted to come to them. I wanted to practically communicate they were not below me in any way and that "I am available". I had a staff member notice and thanked me for that. It's the little things that add up to say, "I am here for you".

Efforts to communicate and demonstrate availability toward your team are not dependent upon anyone's receptivity or agreement. Yet your choice humble leadership. Humble leadership does not constantly point out problems. No place we live, work, or recreate in is lacking in problems. However, only pointing out problems instead of elevating the choices to fix them can sap motivation. If your goal is to be available, avoid being the problem police. Instead, by being approachable you allow your team to have a voice in solving problems.

I have been blessed to serve alongside many wonderful elder teams. I have spent hours and hours with men who love Jesus and His church. However, it has not always been easy serving and leading these teams. Misunderstandings and personalities can linger below the surface if we are not careful. Years ago, one of the elders on our team disagreed with some plans and began to withdraw. We came to realize he was communicating his concerns to others outside the elder team. Of course that is a problem. What was worse when we tried to discuss this situation at our elder meeting this man kept silent? He literally would not say a word. He would not answer any questions even at the pleading of the other elders. In retrospect, I believe he never felt I was approachable, and thus communication broke down. I do believe if I had fostered approachability in more concrete ways he could come to me I feel I could have helped him personally.

Being available and approachable is also seen in not focusing too hard on end results. Everyone likes to focus on continued productivity and growth. Of course that is a goal to have. But helping those you lead focus on effective things they are doing in the present creates a connection. In other words, the process your team engages in matters more. Because it is at the process level personal influence is more likely to occur. Let's dig deeper into this by looking at practical steps toward the fruitful activity of an approachable leader.

Build a healthy culture

As already stated, a large part of building a healthy culture is being available. To communicate availability is to also be approachable. This is easier said than done and will take time and repetition to build and intentionality and resilience to maintain.

I have found there are many little steps that when put together add much to the culture where you work and serve. When the culture is good the possibility of deep impact increases greatly. These efforts, like being available, don't need the permission of anyone. It is a way we serve the whole team. Some may receive your efforts and move toward you and others will remain indifferent. So how do we practically grow our culture? Consider these action points. Each may seem like a small, insignificant step but when you put them all together, they bring health and vitality to the places you work and serve.

- **Style of dress**. It matters. If possible, dress what the average leader/supervisor does in your organization. Avoid the high-priced, newest styles that set you apart in a way that could be construed as superior. When I serve with my church staff, I don't wear a shirt and tie but dress comfortably and is in keeping with the warm atmosphere I am trying to cultivate. When my staff see me around the church during the week I give them no reason to interpret a position of superiority from me. I also don't go the other route and dress sloppy as that communicates disrespect. The bottom line, remove barriers from connecting. So be aware, dress matters.
- **Be a role model at all times**. This means everywhere. In the supermarket, on social media, when communicating with others. In the smaller community of 2000 plus I live in I see my players and those I serve every day. If I show careless behavior in public I undermine my efforts toward personal impact. If you want a warm and inviting atmosphere, you must take the lead in good behavior, communicating in a warm and welcoming manner. I witness firsthand when I coach how the children respond like their dad and mom. If parents yell and complain I have to deal with their kid doing the same thing. As a leader you set an example so set it well. Throughout my coaching career in sports, I do not allow swearing and disrespectful behavior. The player and team will have consequences should they choose those behaviors. Standards matter because behavior matters. Be sure this is modeled and communicated.
- **Work ethic really matters**. Do you respond to messages in a timely fashion? Do you show up when you say you will? People matter and need you to respond appropriately. My Youth director just recently emailed me something she wanted me to look at and give my opinion as to whether it was appropriate to show to the youth. I love the fact she is sensitive to what we teach. I set it on the back burner, and she had to remind me twice. I was convicted of my failure to respond and made her work harder for her. I continually remind myself I need to be prompt and not keep people waiting. To those I lead, no news is bad news. So I must be communicating at all times, in a timely fashion, and not let a vacuum develop where they have to fill in the blanks.
- **Write notes**. Personally encourage and praise through an email or short note. Express gratitude and celebrate the wins. This shows thought and care in a very visual way. I encourage you to buy little "thank you "cards. I have found simple words of gratitude and appreciation for a confident and healthy team.
- **Be punctual**. People who know me know I will start and finish on time whether anyone is there or not. I respect people and their time too much to allow unnecessary fluctuating starting times. A couple of years ago I led a group of about five that oversaw a specific department. We had a meeting, and the others showed up ten minutes late. I had decided on the agenda items and told them the meeting was done and the decisions were made so they could go home. I stuck to it and guess what happened next meeting? Yep, each was about 5-10 minutes early. Over the years I have lost count of how many times I started a meeting or gathering and not everyone had showed yet. But being on time, starting and ending meetings you lead on time shows respect. This contributes to a healthy culture.
- **Speak well of other leaders and supervisors**. Take the lead in speaking well and finding the good to point out. Avoid cutting remarks, gossip, and slander. They have no place on your team. This will eventually flow around the team you lead. The disrespect and ill words about others will plant seeds that will spread throughout the place you lead. No one is perfect and even when there

has been a mistake made be disciplined and speak well of those persons. What a joy to be a part of a team that refuses to entertain cutting and derogatory speech. Having coached many athletic teams over the years I have trained my assistant coaches and teams to speak well of each other. Correction can be communicated in a positive way, but you must stop and control your speech.

- **Run toward those who are conflicted** – We do not like conflict whether we believe to be directly a part of it or not. If you are a leader, you are already a part of it due to our impact on the whole. Run toward those in conflict, not to the conflict. I am in no way saying insert yourself in a conflict or seek to create more but seek to help others handle conflict in a healthy way. This is one of the best ways to build a healthy culture. By not allowing conflict to hijack your teams and your objectives you show love for them.

    Recently I got wind of a woman pulling away from some ministries she was involved in. A part of me wanted to write it off as she was needing a breather but something within me wouldn't let her pull away. I called her as soon as I was able and ran toward her. She was indeed hurting and had assumed some things that were not true. If I had not run toward her she might have alienated herself unnecessarily. This served as another reminder to me to go after those I love and refuse to allow conflict or hurt to fester. I wish I would have done this more often earlier in my life. I believe I allowed unnecessary hurt for dear people because I thought, "O they'll get over it."

    If you go to Colorado and observe how buffalo and cows react to a storm you will notice a stark contrast. When the storms come cows walk away from the storm whereas buffalo walk even charge into the storm. Buffalo somehow know by moving into the storm they shorten the time in the storm.

    We need a buffalo mindset by moving toward challenges and conflicts. Too often we do the opposite. We run away hoping the challenges and conflicts will disappear. This is even more pronounced in our marriages and homes. By avoiding moving toward those with love and grace and seeking clarity and reconciliation if needed we greatly increase the chances of negative consequences and relational distancing. We also extend the length of conflict when not moving towards it.

    No matter what level of your leadership, it is not about you. It is about others. So, move toward conflict and seek to deal with the issues right away. It really comes down to the question of whether you love those you lead enough to do what you are called to do. In those moments listen to what God calls you to do and run towards that.

As you look at the list above you will notice each small step in one way or another communicates the value you place on those you lead. Don't get caught up in formal leadership. To impact others in a personal way requires steps toward personal leadership and healthy cultures come from many small personal leadership efforts.

Be a Coach

No matter who your teams are you have a choice in any and every interaction to put on a coaching hat or a director's hat. Directing may get short-term movement whereas coaches facilitate growth and change that is long-term. To have a deep influence on people's lives requires a coaching mindset.

Being available and building a healthy culture can be done anytime, anywhere, and is directed toward the whole team. Being a coach serves those who want to grow and develop. Unfortunately, not everyone on your team will want to grow. To come alongside others with a coaching approach to a degree requires permission from others to speak into their lives. Your availability opens the door for them to invite you in. Some will be receptive to your offer others will close the door. Whether in a business, organization, church, or team you cannot force others to want to grow. What you can do is identify those who do and offer to come alongside with love, intentionality, and time.

- **Define Coaching**

Coaching those on your teams is a loving investment that involves an intentional partnership designed to help them set, pursue, and reach goals. In the business and organizational realm, it is easy to get locked in on the bottom line and miss the opportunity to help another work toward the goals needed for the business to succeed. A coach enables both reaching the goals and empowering the person through honest feedback, support, inspiration, measured guidance, and motivation. It is to the detriment of both the organization and those who work there if coaching relationships are not present.

To coach those you lead requires authenticity and intentionality. It is easy to seek to get others to work toward what you want or what you see as best but coaching others requires helping them move toward the goals they identify. Coaching them both in identifying those goals and a process to pursue them is both a privilege and a commitment. Depending on your context some of the goals may be part of their position description but in some cases, there should be personal goals as part of your work with them.

When I worked as a supervisor, coached sports teams, and worked with staff in the church setting some of the goals were position-connected, others were joint goals and always some were personal and family goals. Help your people be well-rounded and don't simply focus on the goals that help produce institutional profits. Deep influence seldom happens at the position description level. If you want to have a deep impact, make a deep investment. Even in the workplace the work of grace within you can call out to their deep.

No matter what context, coaching others will require you to be supportive, honest, and available. Being a coach is like being a thought partner. It is wanting the best for others if for no other reason than their growth. I hope you realize the opportunities before you to promote growth, and professional development and deepen others' awareness of God's work in their lives.

- **Coaching variations**

I am a football fan. I love to coach and watch games. A long time ago I loved to play the game. Don Shula was a very successful coach many years ago who led the Miami Dolphins. The players loved playing for him, and it is not hard to know why when you read his philosophy of coaching. He wrote,

"Coaching is not about talent. Or personality. Or Pride. Or ambition. It's about your believing in someone. And then doing whatever it takes to help that person to be his or her very best."

Coaching can be a formal relationship often based on written agreements for results or outcomes. It also can be informal coaching relationships where interactions include coaching elements. What I believe will have the deepest impact is a relationship of trust where the leader seeks to serve another. It comes from the posture of servanthood I talked about in chapter one.

Contextual coaching is sensitive to the context, such as a specific situation or organization. In my context, I could coach others to achieve goals for the church I pastor. I could have my children's ministry coordinator set goals for how she will help the children who come to the church. In this dynamic, I am sensitive to the Church.

Content-loaded coaching relates to a specific use of a product or system. This type of coaching often uses predetermined questions and strategies. For example, a car salesman gets coached in this way. They are trained to approach customers a certain way, share only certain information, and are told parameters when it comes to negotiations. Marketing companies also use this type of coaching.

While those variations are helpful, they are business accomplishment-oriented. The coaching I am referring to is heart-directed coaching. The heart of a leader calls out to another what is within them.

As I have said, I love to coach sports and within that, I try to coach hearts. That is to seek to pull out of them the issues of the heart. In the teenage years issues of identity, belonging and fear are in the forefront of their minds. They are also issues of the heart. So I want to seek to spend time bringing these issues up in both group practice and one-on-one. How do I do that?

If I say anything that would be of most help to you it would be this. Become a master at asking questions. Questions that help others identify their real thoughts, obstacles that they perceive, and goals and dreams.

It would be helpful to clarify coaching others is not counseling others. Counseling tends to focus on the past and present. Counselors work to understand, facilitate healing, and bring resolutions to problems. Coaching instead focuses on the present and future. It leads to action and achievement. Coaching has a proactive and creative leaning.

Mentoring is a popular term being used. Mentoring, like coaching, is relationship based resulting in life application and knowledge. The focus is life-on-life modeling. They are different and the differences matter and should be noted. While mentors share their successes and learnings. Coaches focus on drawing out others' successes and learnings. Simply put mentors pour their best into others, and coaches pull the best out of others. It is this "pulling" that creates a deep-on-deep impact.

The author of Proverbs speaks to this "Though good advice lies deep within the heart, a person with understanding will draw it out." Proverbs 20:5 (NLT)

Years ago, I worked at a wood manufacturing plant and was a supervisor in the veneer department. I oversaw and worked with a team of men and women, young and old, and varied ethnicities. I enjoyed working with them. I worked to build relationships with each other and sought to build a team that knew and cared for each other. There was one young man, Dan, who I worked alongside. I began to go deeper within conversations and asked him many questions to help him as he sought direction. He would pull me aside between shifts and call me to talk about life. I knew God was allowing this relationship to be one where I could help Dan move from where he was to where he believed God wanted him to be. Dan was not a Christian when we first met. I shared the good news of Jesus' love and grace with him, and he was receptive. He talked with me before he proposed to his girlfriend and many other issues. I also worked on the same machine as he did, and I left passages of the Bible I was trying to memorize sitting on the platform where the controls were. He would often comment on them. I came alongside Dan and helped him discover God's agenda for his life. That is coaching. Although in a secular workplace, I still was able to speak into another's life in a deep way.

After Dan moved on to take over another department God brought me a man named Louis. I came alongside him in a similar way I did Dan. As a leader, you have an opportunity with those you lead to do that.

Have you ever thought of investing in others' lives as a gift to them? I hope to challenge you to look beyond just showing up at work, doing your job, and going home. Look around where you work and ask God who you can come alongside and begin to invest in their life, serve them by coaching them.

- **Basic Coaching Principles**

Let's get practical as to how you can begin or deepen your interactions with people you desire to come alongside. I have found leaders who coach effectively share these characteristics:

➢ Leaders/coaches are intuitive listeners
➢ Leaders/coaches are authentic encouragers
➢ Leaders/coaches are powerful questioners
➢ Leaders/coaches are focused, direct, and trustworthy
➢ Leaders/coaches are compassionate

Read these over again slowly. Measure your leadership with your teams against these principles. If you are like me there is at least one that grabs your attention as being deficient in your interactions. I need to remind myself over and over to shut up and listen. The impatient and sinful part of me wants to give the quick answer and move on. Integrating these characteristics provides clarity and sets others on a forward and fruitful course.

In his work called *Masterful Coaching,* Robert Hargrove spoke to this idea of *deep influence through coaching.*

"The key to becoming a master coach lies in having the dream, aspiration, and the bone-deep commitment to make a difference in the lives, groups, or entire organizations…Coaching is about challenging and supporting people, giving them the gift of your presence."

I encourage you to process the following principles to implement into how you help guide and coach those in your home or organization. I have found the below acronym as a helpful guide to memorize to help guide those you are working with. I draw upon it when working with others.

- **"Learn" others**

If you want to have a deep influence in people's lives "learn" them! Taking a coaching posture with others requires intentional efforts/actions. These efforts when regularly practiced become skills. The

Coaching Center years ago made the L.E.A.R.N. diagram which illustrated the relative use of skills used in coaching conversations.[1]

The acronym broke the main skills of coaching down like this.

Listen
Encourage
Ask
Respond
Navigate

While these efforts serve as a good guide for one-on-one coaching interactions, I have found them helpful in stopping and determining where conversations may be leading. Think of your teams and where interactions both scheduled and unscheduled with these individuals take place. Consider how these might help. I'd like to make some comments on each point for they are incredibly helpful to you in leading those you love.

Listening is one of, if not the most, needed skill. To listen means we become engaged and focused. To do this remove distractions, don't interrupt. Be sensitive to tone and body posture. Discern what they are saying.

Encouraging others authentically needs to be a part of our coaching efforts. The word encourage means to instill courage. I find that definition helpful. People blossom and thrive when they are encouraged. Most people do not get near enough encouragement in their lives. How can we do this among our teams? Support with words such as, "I know you got this" or "I know you have the courage to take this risk". Use your words to support. Speak hope and always speak hope. We live in a "Debbie Downer" world and your people need hope. Send encouraging notes. Communicate the potential you see and commend them for the growth you have seen.

Asking questions can be powerful. Questions help foster needed mental shifts in those we come alongside. Powerful questions are precise and clarifying. For example,

What do you know so far?
Where do you want to go? What is your desired outcome?
What are you wanting to see accomplished?
Where are you in the process?
What part of what you are doing brings you the most joy?
What is the first or next step you need to take?
What will need to happen for you to have a sense of completion?
What do you sense God is saying to you?
What resources do you need?

These questions lead to specificity regarding forward progress. Open-ended questions such as, '" tell me about that" do not help progress. Ask specific powerful questions. In doing so you help those you love to count the cost, identify challenges and obstacles, see with vision, surface beliefs, reflect on the meaning of relationships, and discover motivations of the heart. Those are significant results. Asking great questions serves others well.

Respond with reality. In my experience, this seems to be a transactional point between questions and actions. Responding to those we come alongside is like holding a mirror up for them to reflect back on what they have discovered and shared. It is important to help them stay in a non-anxious place at this point especially. You are reviewing and clarifying. This helps them identify inconsistencies and reaffirm where God may be leading them. Responding to others involves sharing truth, honest feedback, and acknowledging God's guidance.

Navigate by allowing the actions to be named. Help determine action steps. Remove obstacles and call them to give voice to what they are willing to do. And when they will do it, always navigate people to their unique abilities and skills. Navigation requires accountability.

Dan Reiland in his excellent book "Confident Leader" speaks to ways we can help navigate our people. He writes, *" It's always best to focus on a leader's strengths, but there are times when you must invest time in his or her struggles."*

He goes on to give an effective picture for assessment to determine *"their zone"*. Here is how he assesses.

- *Strength zone = They are swimming well, and making progress.*
- *Struggle zone =They are treading water, just maintaining.*
- *Stuck zone = They are going under, in danger of drowning.*[2]

I love this for it emphasizes the purpose of assessment which is to help others to move beyond the hindrances of progress and build on their strengths. Navigating others is about guiding others to realize this.

Because this process of coaching is personal drawing out and learning the individuals in your departments or teams requires being sensitive to the atmosphere in which you meet. Years ago, I had the privilege to serve with John, a youth pastor. John is an incredibly loving and gifted man. We would meet weekly in my office and go through the ministry schedule and particular challenges and plans. When I first stepped into my position as expected he was somewhat reserved when it came to sharing and talking through the challenges he was facing. As I sought to listen, come alongside, and guide him into greater ministry effectiveness we would get to a point where he would stop the interaction. It was like he would close the blinds both in tone and body language.

I made two decisions. One I would spend time each meeting drawing out what he was passionate about and past dreams he had in his younger years. He felt safe with these topics and began to share freely. After some time his sharing became more personal.

Secondly, I decided to go to his office when we met instead of mine. I noticed his comfort level was greater when I came to him. He began to open up and we were able to talk through the tough decisions we faced, and personal prayer times became richer and more in-depth. I learned it was the small steps of allowing him to share at his level and speed and going to him on "his turf" that made a big difference. So, I have tried to do that regularly. Taking these steps alone removes one potential obstacle in coaching those on my team. Maybe the individuals you are seeking to work with don't have an office instead look for other locations that would be warmer to meet with those you are coaching.

I have learned over the years that achievement can subtly sneak in and undermine our efforts to coach others toward their best. Yes, growing our organizations and achieving success both in measurable progress and productivity is important and necessary. But these must not become so dominant they begin to change the way we think and prioritize. We cannot allow ourselves to drift from a coaching mindset to a corporate board mindset. We cannot allow ourselves to replace a humble, approachable manner with a static, impersonal one.

The cultivation of deep influence in others' lives does not happen by accident. It takes sustained commitment. The joy of seeing others grow and achieve what they never thought possible is worth the effort needed. Even more the opportunity to lead others out of grace toward grace can bring eternal results.

Be intentional in showing you are available, build a healthy culture, and coach up those on your team who show a desire to grow. As you put forth these efforts out of a heart filled with grace you can be assured of truly helping others move toward God's best.

CHAPTER SIX

Leading Through Trials

It was very early one morning when I was about 5 or 6 years old that I was awakened by a noise outside my bedroom door. All the bedrooms for us six kids and my parent's room in our house were upstairs. I heard several voices and feet moving up and down the stairs. The sounds grew louder and the voices more numerous. Voices I did not recognize. Although fearful, curiosity took me to the bedroom door where I peeked out into the hallway. There were several men in uniforms with a bed on rollers and my mom was laying on it. Dad was there talking with the men and following them down the stairs. Dad looked at me and said go back to bed and it will be okay.

I heard Dad talking to my older sisters about watching us all. I did not find out until the morning that my mom had a stroke caused by an aneurysm. That night changed our family in many ways. My sisters' roles changed, and they had to grow up fast to take on the role of caretaker. My little sister and I couldn't quite grasp the seriousness of what was happening. Nor the long-term changes that were coming.

My mom would pull through yet would face months of speech and physical therapy. It was during the months and years that followed I watched my dad lead our family through this crisis. I am sure if you asked each of my siblings about those days they would share the impact from their perspective and experiences. We did share, through the crisis, the commonality of fear, uncertainty, and loss. Loss regarding our normal way of life and in some ways mom's normal which was safe and comforting. Now we as six siblings faced an uncertain future.

We also shared the experience of living under Dad's leadership through this. I never appreciated how Dad led through this all until years later when my siblings would share about those times. The disruption Mom's stroke caused in our home was major, but somehow Dad kept organization, consistency, and even more importantly hope in our family. I saw what delegation looked like as Dad made adjustments, laid out responsibilities, and sought to calm the fears.

Dad also led in such a way that we were unaware of the financial hardship that was created by the medical costs. His attitude brought a settling dynamic to us all. I know he truly wanted us to enjoy our childhood, and I know, as he shared with me later in life, the difficulty for him in watching how hard it affected us all. Dad showed me a lot about how to face trials. Equally important he showed me some ways to lead those I love through trials. The opportunity to have a deep impact is multiplied when we journey through trials well.

I want you to consider how you will lead through your own personal trials. I am discovering a decreasing number of people know how to journey well through trials and crises. Much less leading others in the midst of the trials. Too many begin to lose their identity and go day to day with a defeatist attitude. They move from normal functioning to losing themselves in the trials. Walking through trials in a healthy way means we do not allow them to rob us of joy, hope, and peace. We refuse to allow the trial to detour us from purposeful and passionate living. To walk through the trials in a healthy way requires honesty and a receptive heart. Open to the healing and strengthening flow of God's grace.

Some would confess they feel ill-prepared to live a life of perseverance. For many, there is a shortage of joy and hope. For others, it is a lack of direction. Whatever the reason, walking through the upheavals in life with passion and purpose appears out of reach. It can be frustrating seeking to achieve what we would like when confronted with trials. We need help and hope. We cannot lose our self, our identity, our purpose in the storms of life. And we cannot leave behind others who need our leadership when the trials come.

We need direction and perspective personally and we need to give these to those we lead. It is especially in the storms and trials that we discover we have much to learn and much to impart.

We need trials. For within them lie treasures that provide us wisdom and focus to live life abundantly along with authentic honesty and perseverance to make a deep impact. An absence of struggle is not evidence we are maximizing life. A joy-filled and impacting life is forged from the challenges life brings. God never wastes anything that comes our way. He will always use circumstances in life for the good if we surrender to His ways. It bears repeating that we need to be honest and receptive at the heart level to both grow and lead.

It is my sincere desire the lessons I have learned, and shared will help you in your journey and leadership. Malcolm Muggeridge once said: *"Every parable, great and small, is a parable whereby God speaks to us; and the art is to get the message."*

I don't want to waste any trials, but to hear the messages they send and learn the lessons they contain. The psalmist in the Bible, *"It was good for me to be afflicted so that we may learn your ways."* (Psalm 119:71 NIV)

Can you say that about your trials? "It was good"? The good is that the psalmist was able to learn about the ways of God he could not have learned any other way. It is in the trials the work of grace does its most penetrating work.

When we can echo the words of the psalmist we have begun to walk through our trials in a healthy way. For whatever has come our way, God has not, and is not, wasting anything. He won't waste your circumstances nor the opportunities to help others.

All our stories indwell God's story making our lives part of a grand plan. Even our trials fall within that grand plan. I believe we can experience and see the hand of God at work in our stories. And in how we help others in theirs. Leading others through their trials primarily is done by walking through ours before them authentically. So how do we do that?

Consider your trials

A passage from the New Testament book of James gives us a perspective to hold regarding facing the trials in life:

"Consider it pure joy, my brothers and sisters, whenever you face trials of many kinds, because you know that the testing of your faith produces perseverance. Let perseverance finish its work so that you may be mature and complete, not lacking anything." (James 1:2-4 NIV)

The word "Consider "means to "give careful thought to". It carries the idea of reflecting on something. This is the word James uses in reference to how to view unexpected events. I have taken James' words to heart and considered my trials and surprises. Here is my conviction and desire: God has not called me to just survive the storms and surprises in life. God wants me to embrace the purposes of my trials. This requires building a deep, abiding sense that God is in the storms; in control of the storms, purposeful in the storms, and good in all He does and allows. All of those convictions are wrapped up in the word "consider."

How are you considering your trials? How have you responded to the jolt of surprises? Now might be a good time to consider those questions. All through the Bible, God has a call for His people. It is a call to follow Him wherever that journey may lead.

Over and over, we see examples of people who walked in faith and journeyed with enduring joy. Hebrews 11 tells the story of those who followed God and led others in the midst of challenges. I encourage you to read the chapter. You will be reminded, by the examples portrayed, that we are not called to simply survive the trials and surprises in life. Instead, we are to rise up and live out God's call on our lives in the midst of the trials. This call is not to be comfortable, but to serve God and grow in Christlikeness. It's not to hide and run from every trial but to be an authentic light to others amid the trials. We are called to journey on the path set before us, including the trials, authentically and joyfully.

I know in the quietness of our hearts, we wrestle with all the uncertainties, fear, and pain that trials can unmask. Walking through the surprises can seem unbearable. However, they also can be enlightening, if we consider them rightly. I know from my experiences I have wondered at times if I was up for the challenges much less leading others in the midst of them.

Along with my mom's stroke, as a young boy, I experienced several seizures and was subsequently diagnosed with Epilepsy. Leukemia, colorectal cancer, and cancer metastasis to my left lung and liver would also visit my world. Each trial is unique in its specific challenges and impact.

As I, along with Cyndy and the kids, have tried to come to grips with my cancer, we faced decisions we felt ill-prepared to make. We were told there would need to be radiation, chemo treatments, and then surgery. With our heads spinning after the original cancer diagnosis, we focused on educating ourselves about whether we would agree with the prescribed treatments. That calmness felt so fragile. The waves seemed relentless and suffocating. The consequences of leukemia, cancers, and surgeries have affected to a degree my quality of living today. The changes all began with a surprising announcement of cancer. Talk about a jolt. Let's be honest, cancer is a scary word.

After my first cancer surgery, we had just settled into a routine of doctor checkups. At one such appointment, Cyndy and I were planning our day as we waited for the doctor to come and report blood count numbers as usual. We were about to be hit with another surprise. The Cancer had returned.

It was at this point I gained a greater urgency in trying to prepare Cyndy and the kids for the possibility of not making it through this cancer. God was telling me to not despair or complain but to lead. The doctor was sober with the news, and it was not hard to grasp that metastasis is bad news. To be honest, more than any fear that may have been present was a nagging thought I hadn't done enough to prepare Cyndy and the kids.

God used Bible verses to give me insight into what was happening from heaven's perspective. I began to consider these questions: Could it be God was going to use cancer to teach me His ways? To strengthen and develop me? Were the circumstances that appeared worthless actually treasures? Was God giving me an opportunity to lead others toward the grace of God?

I grew in the belief that God would not waste anything, and if I could journey through in a healthy way, I would discover insights that would be invaluable and lead in ways that could be transformational. From my journey, I want to continue to learn and share lessons God has taught, and my experiences have confirmed.

Consider your trials my friend and learn the ways of God that will enable you to journey purposefully, passionately, and even joyfully. These are some of the treasures that await those seeking to learn and lead amidst life's challenges.

Leverage your trials

I want to make a connection regarding living authentically and leading out of your trials. You will waste your trials and lose yourself in them if you do not face them honestly. If we will face them honestly and authentically, we will find trials produce opportunities to impact lives like never before. As I mentioned in another chapter how important dads are in their children's lives. This importance is magnified when our families have an opportunity to watch how to walk through trials in a healthy way. It is one thing to read a verse from the Bible to my kids about trials and quite another to apply and live out that verse.

It was a powerful moment when I realized what I was facing provided me an opportunity to model and teach what I could not apart from the cancer. It was in those moments of clarity I began to say to myself often, "Don't waste your cancer". I knew to do this I would have to be vulnerable and genuine. Free from the false fronts. Because inauthenticity weakens influence. Facing trials squarely allows us to leverage them for teaching and modeling. At the core of a life that has a deep influence is grace and grace is on display when the trials show up. The author of the Book of James says that God gives a greater grace. Greater than all our trials and greater than our weaknesses. His is a never-ending supply of mercy.

I don't want to be a shallow person who glosses over the real heart and mind issues that emerge in life and its challenges. I want to journey well and help others journey well. To be able to do that I need to make the most of my trials.

I was leafing through one of my journals from over ten years ago and came upon this quote from A.B. Sampson, *"Allow God time to work and He surely will. Then the very trials that threatened to overcome you with discouragement and disaster will become God's opportunity to reveal His grace and glory in your life in ways you've never known before"*.

I have and am learning what Sampson speaks of. What a gift God gives the honest seeker. Life-changing lessons await the receptive heart. The lasting impact flows from a surrendered life. The pain of your pilgrimage can bring healing and hope to others. It can be a source for you to feed your loved ones, to feed them in terms of character, to fuel their growth and development.

Draw near to God through the questions

Before being able to truly lead in the midst of personal trials one must face and process the trials in an honest way. As a matter of fact, this honest journey is part of the curriculum for you to grow in leading others. Without a doubt, questions are birthed in the trials. Not facing them slows our growth. We are limited in our impact and sidetracked in regard to our calling. Freedom, confidence, and convictions that can develop will elude us if we don't face the questions the storms bring. God is tender in allowing us to raise questions in our intimate moments with Him. Lest we feel praying to God is a dumping and whining activity, the Bible points out that prayer is as much if not more listening to God. In this, the questions invite us nearer to God. Many in the Bible wrestled with questions about what God allowed to come into their lives. Job, the prophets Habakkuk and Jonah, and King David to name a few.

Questions are part of our journey – they were and are part of mine. They were a part of King David's journey as well. This is clear from Psalm 13, where we read this short prayer of David.

1 How long, Lord? Will You forget me forever? How long will You hide your face from me? 2 How long must I wrestle with my thoughts and day after day have sorrow in my heart? How long will my enemy triumph over me? 3 Look on me and answer, Lord my God. Give light to my eyes, or I will sleep in death, 4 and my enemy will say, "I have overcome him," and my foes will rejoice when I fall. 5 But I trust in Your unfailing love; my heart rejoices in Your salvation. 6 I will sing the Lord's praise, for He has been good to me." (NIV)

Interestingly enough, the psalm cannot be confidently connected to any specific event in David's life. All attempts to place it are but guesses. An "enemy" is mentioned, but no further evidence is given. Some believe David was very ill at this time. Whatever the circumstances, we find him disoriented from the upheaval in his life.

This reflective psalm expresses the feelings of this man and of those who face life's storms. I find it comforting to be in the dark as to the background of this psalm as it allows me to fill in my trial and face my questions. I really can't learn the essence of David's psalm until it becomes mine.

Psalm 13 is a unique prayer. There are questions in this psalm as well the process by which to approach them. I find the model incredibly helpful and freeing. In the psalm, the word choices are instructive. The question, "How long?" is used four times. This repetition emphasizes the intensity of the emotions. There is a progressive element in verse 3 seen in the verb choices. "Look on", "answer" and then "give light". All speak to the ongoing experience of honest prayer. The request for God to consider, answer, and enlighten becomes a turning point in the psalmist's prayer, as it will in ours. If the psalmist had stopped after the question "How long?", depression and discouragement would have prevailed. But he wrestled on in his prayer. He wrestled honestly. As he did, God brought greater clarity and assurance.

The prayers of the psalmist and many of the prophets in the Bible are neither flowery nor contrived. What they are is honest. If you haven't prayed this way yet, there are some lessons concerning prayer that are coming your way. I have and am asking questions in my prayers. In my prayer life, I have found when I ask questions of God I can simultaneously wonder if the presence of the questions signals I am buckling under the fears and uncertainties. When facing leukemia and cancer surgeries, many questions surfaced. "How long" questions have been part of my prayers. How long do I have left on this earth?

How long do I have left with the love of my life Cyndy? Will I be able to walk Angela and Emily down the aisle for their weddings? How will Cyndy get by if I don't make it? Have I done enough to point my children to Jesus? Do I have the inner strength to make it through this without crashing emotionally? Will I slip back into the struggle with the loneliness I periodically have faced over the years? Yes, there was and is no shortage of questions.

After my cancer metastasized to my lung and the subsequent lobectomy, I returned from the hospital still in much pain. The painkillers and ibuprofen were bringing limited relief. One day I began to get a fever, and with my leukemia, this is always a concern. When we called the doctor, I was told to go to the emergency room at a local hospital. The X-rays revealed a large amount of fluid next to the surgery site. The local doctor called Mayo Clinic late that night with the results and discussed my condition and how to proceed. The Mayo doctors expressed concern and wanted me taken there immediately in case things went south quickly. It was after midnight when I was rolled into an ambulance and taken to the Mayo Clinic in Rochester. In the quiet and darkness of the rainy night, I experienced deep loneliness. The two hours in the back of the ambulance had me wondering why I could not get past the onslaught of health issues. Why did I also have to face the pain of loneliness again? I knew there were paramedics in the ambulance, but they clearly did not want to have a conversation with me beyond a medical question. I confess I felt very alone. In reality, I knew God was there, but I did not sense He was there. He seemed so removed from me at that moment. My prayer in the back of that ambulance consisted of desperate and ignorant words. But I prayed. And I was honest. I believe God heard those prayers. At that moment, that was all I knew.

We can learn in our walk with God, that certain experiences will bring us to places where our prayers meet our fears and desperation. I am finding more and more; this type of honest prayer is the avenue to real change. This is true in my life. It's not that anything necessarily changes in regard to my circumstances. I still have cancer. I still lost part of my lower colon, most of my lungs, and part of my liver, and still face colon challenges. The consequences of the several surgeries haven't changed. But I have. And I am. I know it is because God has met me in the questions and the honest moments with Him. Honestly facing the questions before God has brought growth.

I am learning that getting to the place where I live with a deep peace often involves wrestling in prayer with the questions. A deep, gut-level prayer that can sound anything but spiritual. I know that Jesus will find me in those confusing, uneasy places. I just don't want to be in those places. God may choose to heal the outer afflictions or calm the inner me. Either is fine, as long as I am near to Him.

I never cease to be amazed at how God can use our struggles. Because of the battle with cancer, God opened the door for me and Cyndy to share the lessons and the message of God's love in many ways. We have been on TV shows in Atlanta and Pittsburgh. We have shared our journey on radio shows, podcasts, and written publications. I have been asked to share at men's retreats and other events. God opened those doors and when those opportunities came, I believed God reminded me "I am using these trials. Don't waste your cancer, Matt".

As you wrestle with these thoughts, you may be thinking, "My gosh, I could never share my thoughts with anyone, much less tell God what I think." The good news is, God invites you to share honestly. He rewards those who do seek Him genuinely. In fact, it is in prayer you will find the peace and hope you need to press on. Don't quit. Talk with God often and honestly.

For those who read this and are facing desperate times, I encourage you to take your questions and fears to God in prayer. For the "atheist" who is struggling mentally, seeking to reconcile a God and His level of involvement with the trials that have come. For the widow who now sets a table for one. For the child who no longer comes home to two parents. For the one who has made big-time mistakes and day after day carries big-time regrets. For the mom and dad who have lost a child. For anyone who feels like life is falling apart. I offer this to you. Be honest in prayer. This is the first step toward real growth and healing. The ache and problems won't disappear. The circumstances might not change. But you will change. For this kind of honest prayer will lead you to a place of experiencing God's love and grace in a personal way and make possible a deep, miraculous, and abiding peace.

Like living authentically day to day, walking through your personal trials in an honest way earns you the right to be heard.

Refresh your spirit

Trials sap strength in more ways than one. Physical, mental, emotional, and spiritual vitality is threatened the longer and more intense the trials. I certainly have found that to be true. Yet I know that is not God's desire. Trials while difficult and exhausting do not need to have the final word on how we live our day-to-day lives. I have found the following action steps to be helpful to refresh my mind and spirit. I keep this list available to remind myself and hope they can be of help to you.

1. Acknowledge my sinfulness. By this, I mean confessing my neediness for God's grace and strength. I sometimes try to select the more spiritual-sounding words and act with a fabricated persona. I have learned to be quick to acknowledge the ways I depend on my abilities and not His grace. As a Christian refreshing myself in the gospel is a must.
2. Downsize my word output. Few know how to ask questions of others and how to seek what God may be saying in other people's experiences. When I lay in the hospital beds after my cancer surgeries, I made it my goal to engage the nurses and doctors, ask them how they were, and seek to listen to them. Because the questions were always focused on me "How do you feel" I did not want my condition and circumstances to be about me more than they had to be. Trials along with the related challenges can take us to the empty places of self-absorption. I also need to work hard at not telling my staff, teams, and others my latest insights and opinions about everything. I'm not quite as smart as I think and saying less is better. When I do this, I find something freeing within me.
3. Focus my day – Through Bible reading, journaling, and prayer I try to leave with a focus for the day. I seek to grab hold of a truth God has highlighted. Like the banks of a river, it helps me channel my energies in the right direction.
4. Receive God's love – This certainly includes refreshing myself in the gospel but also sitting before my Father as His child. It is conversing with Him in intimate ways and sitting still and listening to the rhythms of His heart. My children used to sit on my lap when they were young and put their heads on my chest. Eventually, they all would at some point say "I can hear your heartbeat dad". That is the posture that refreshes my spirit. To rest and hear the heartbeat of God through His Spirit and His Word. No easy thing with my so often distracted mind.

5. Renounce fixing as a way of life. First off not everything is a problem. I am not called either to fix every problem or person. Nor do I need to weigh in on every problem. This allows me to laugh more and make sure my enthusiasm is higher.
6. Spend time with weak and hurting people. Loving people well will always bring God's favor and peace. Make this a priority to more time with those you are closest to. Be a friend to the broken and find God brings a corresponding peace.
7. Take walks and rest in the quiet. I know some who put worship music in their air buds and simply sing to the Lord as they walk. This is an awesome way to regain perspective and enjoy God's presence. In the quietness, we are most able to hear that small still voice of the Spirit.

I do not do these as often as I should, nor do I go down through the list to cover every action. I do use the actions to take intentional steps to refresh my spirit when trials assault my body, mind, and heart.

The apostle Paul experienced a degree of trials few have. Here is his testimony about God's work in His trials;

But he said to me, "My grace is sufficient for you, for my power is made perfect in weakness." Therefore I will boast all the more gladly about my weaknesses, so that Christ's power may rest on me. That is why, for Christ's sake, I delight in weaknesses, in insults, in hardships, in persecutions, in difficulties. For when I am weak, then I am strong.
2 Corinthians 12:9-11

Note the connection of experiencing God's grace in his hardships. If we want deep influence, which as I have stated throughout comes from an overflow of the work of grace in our lives, hardships provide great opportunities.

A continual refreshing of your spirit will enable you to lead well through the trials. Don't waste your trials. Allow God to use them in your life to grow you and your influence.

CHAPTER SEVEN

Leading Through the Fog

The world has become increasingly chaotic and volatile. Morals are flung out the window, entitlement abounds, and trust is fragile. Leaders are looked at with skepticism and a pervasive distrust and rebellious spirits continue to grow throughout the population. To add to the moral and spiritual fog is the pressure to lead people through all the uncertainties and obstacles. I have learned that leadership is like the tide. When it rises, everything else rises with it.

I was in high school when my parents decided to move from Crystal Lake, Illinois to a small town in Wisconsin. We had relatives who lived in Wisconsin and my dad found property down the road from them with a barn on it. Being the visionary my dad was he decided he would turn the barn into a home. So, for two years we worked on the renovation over weekends. One Sunday in the winter we left the Wisconsin property to head back to Illinois and upon leaving the weather was uneventful with no precipitation. As we progressed heavy snow began and the wind picked up considerably. By the time we were a few miles from the border of Illinois, we could not see the road. We could not see five yards in front of the car. We saw no lights anywhere. We were in a dangerous situation.

Dad stopped the car and put on his flashers, although I doubt anyone could see them. My uncle and I got out and walked several feet ahead of our car to determine we were on the road and free from hitting any structures. It appeared we were out in the middle of nowhere and could not see to get somewhere.

We concluded someone would need to get in the road ahead of the car and walk to make sure we stayed on the road. This required us to push snow away to find concrete on the road. Due to the heavy wind, we rotated every couple of minutes who was leading the car. Eventually, a light became visible, and we led the car toward the light which happened to be a bar. Being a Sunday night, it was closed but we found the owner's house next door and were thankful they were home and let us wait the storm out in the bar.

When I consider leading through the times we live in that memory surfaces. The visibility in that storm was zero which made direction difficult to discern and progress near impossible. The conditions brought decisions with serious consequences. The conditions required someone to lead through the lack of visibility.

Likewise, through the difficulty of challenges, your teams will face, there will be a need for a leader. A leader who is courageous enough to walk in front of their family or teams. There is a good chance you have faced those times, and you did not know the next step you should take. You felt like your family or team was heading off the road and you scrambled for a solution. Relationships became strained, focus was lost, and momentum came to a screeching halt. Whether in your marriage, home, or office a leader is needed to move through the challenging and confusing times.

Decision-making, problem-solving, conflict resolution, and planning can become incredibly difficult at those times. It is exactly these things leaders need to address strategically if they are to provide solid leadership in these times. Can we lead in such an unstable and cloudy atmosphere? How do we handle the relational and communication breakdowns? If it is possible, where do we start?

Several years ago, I pastored a church that was growing and vibrant. A concern was brought to our elder board on a doctrinal issue. We as leaders discussed the concern but did not feel it was a major issue but something we would research more and keep an eye on. Soon there was a larger group expressing the concern which then turned into questioning of others' beliefs, motives, and character. The original concern seemed to be fed and talked about to the degree in the minds of some the church was infected with false teaching. The elders discerned this was not the case. Opposing groups were formed, many relationships became strained, personal discipleship was questioned, judgements of motives emerged, and leadership was doubted and attacked. Large congregational meetings became platforms where personal opinions were launched like missiles. The weird part is it seemed to come out of nowhere.

As the leadership continued interacting with the issue and related concerns we studied the teachings related to the issue, consulted national leaders for counsel, met multiple times with dissenters, and prayed. And prayed!

Unfortunately, a large group left due to their displeasure with how leadership handled things. I have thought long and hard about those times. While my heart grieves at all the pain, confusion, and hurt caused. There was confusion and fog that developed around the ministry. In the midst of all that the elder board rose to the occasion. We did not do everything perfectly but what we did provided a way for the whole church to have a path we could all walk together out of the fog. Looking back, I see God's hand in leading us.

Aside from seeking to meet with dissenters we made some strategic decisions and took some steps that made a difference. I saw my role as helping process and coach the elder board so we together would provide leadership. With our hearts and prayers united we moved forward with discernment. While we never made a "to-do" list per se we did identify and commit to some intentional steps. These steps as I look back were exactly what was needed and because of that, I know those elders would share my perspective that God led us. There were moments it was hard to see through the confusion that resulted and hard to lead through the strain in personal relationships. We knew we were the ones to get in front and lead through the storm.

I share these action steps we took because I see how they helped us lead through the fog. After the dissenting group left and we moved forward with these steps the Church developed a deep unity and growth became marked. This unity and growth allowed us to move forward and seek God together. We made several big decisions, including building over a four-million-dollar new facility, refocusing staff, and a church name change. All in less than two years' time. I believe the steps we took provided direction and are also transferrable. These steps will also allow you to move out of the fog into greater clarity and growth. I know they will be of help to you as you lead your marriage, family, team, or organization out of times when the visibility is low, chaos and uncertainty reign

Make the relational investment of a leader

In the midst of all the confusion the elders and I met with various dissenters and those who were discouraged and, in some cases, attacked. Once again, I give credit to the elders who demonstrated shepherd's hearts when meeting with people in a patient and personal way. At times we dealt with people as a father would a child. Like Paul did with some churches. Tender when needed and firm at other times. There were times we had to call people on the carpet for unacceptable and unbiblical behaviors. There were tears, frustration, repentance, and much prayer as we met with people. There were times we met with others with a counseling mindset. The elders all did a great job of taking a listening posture and seeking to serve. We focused on relationships and leading our people to respond in healthy ways. I remember doing some teaching on what the Bible says about relational health around that time.

As I have studied the life of Jesus I have found the perfect leader. So, who better to learn how to lead from? In His life on earth, he called twelve to follow Him. They were a diverse group in many ways. Scripture especially highlights their personalities, temperaments, and struggles. Yet Jesus chose them to invest His life into. What I find even more amazing is he chose three to invest in at an even deeper level. Peter, James, and John were Jesus' key people He invested in. As I look at Jesus' actions from a leadership perspective I see four actions, He modeled for me and you.

He taught, prayed, loved, and gave time. Jesus listened and when necessary corrected. Simply put He invested in each man. He had a ministry of presence. You cannot lead people in a way that produces more leaders if you do not know and love them. To invest in people requires time.

After Jesus rose from the dead and ascended into heaven the men Jesus invested His life into soon would stand and face thousands of new believers and the growing needs that accompanied them. Can you imagine the thoughts they had and the challenges they faced? I am sure they were totally overwhelmed yet they had Jesus' words and example entrusted to them.

It took time for Jesus to pour into these men's lives. It took His presence with them. Jesus was intentional with them and wasted no opportunities to teach and encourage. A wedding, funeral, worship service, or breakfast on a beach. He taught among those considered most sinful, despised, and useless. These untouchables and outcasts he served became the curriculum in which he taught grace and mercy. He told the disciples to serve those considered the least was to serve Him. Here is the connection with the posture of a servant. You cannot truly invest in a life if you have not served them. This is true in the home, workplace, or on the field of play.

If you desire to build into others' lives, serve them. Keep serving them. Be attentive to ways that would bless them and show your love for them beyond what they can do for you. Invest time and energy in serving and praying for them.

The Apostle Paul demonstrated a personal investment in people's lives when we read his words to a church in the town of Thessalonica.

> *Instead, we were like young children among you. Just as a nursing mother cares for her children, so we cared for you. Because we loved you so much, we were delighted to share with you not only the gospel of God but our lives as well. Surely you remember, brothers and sisters, our toil and hardship; we worked night and day in order not to be a burden to anyone while we preached the gospel of God to you. You are witnesses, and so is God, of how holy, righteous and blameless we*

were among you who believed. For you know that we dealt with each of you as a father deals with his own children, encouraging, comforting and urging you to live lives worthy of God, who calls you into his kingdom and glory. 1 Thessalonians 2:7-12(NIV)

That passage, and the whole letter of 1 Thessalonians for that matter, shouts "personal engagement required for impact". Paul's impact was powerful because it was personal. Paul's leadership, like Jesus', was marked by relational investment.

I have had a unique ministry pathway. I began pastoring at Faith EFC in Stanley, Wisconsin and after about ten years we moved a couple of hours away and pastored a church for about 6 years and then moved over to serve a church west of Minneapolis. The church in Stanley asked me to come back and serve as their pastor. Serving a much smaller church than what I was pastoring in Minnesota, became more realistic for me as I battled cancer. My energy level made serving the precious larger church family in Minnesota difficult. So God took me back to where it all began Faith EFC in Stanley. I have been blessed to serve with wonderfully encouraging and godly people in each of the churches. I have been blessed to know, serve alongside, and mentor numerous elders and staff. I mostly look back and rejoice but a few times cringe.

One such cringe moment has to do with this area of relational investment. The church I was pastoring at the time was pursuing changes on a couple of fronts. Without going into too much detail to avoid missing the point, conflict arose among certain ministry leaders, and it seemed I was right in the middle of each of the issues. I wish I knew then what I know now but I didn't. I believed that the relational trust that I had built years earlier with people would carry us through the difficult times. What I failed to do was to continue to invest in deepening relationships with the people I found myself butting heads with. I erroneously thought because me and some others related well in the past that automatically the trust would be there when conflict hit. Over time the tension and conflict built without any intentional relationship-building efforts being made. Without efforts to build up relationships the table was set for breakdowns in communication and the enemy to place seeds of distrust in our hearts. My defensiveness, immaturity, and ignorance really contributed to a difficult time. By God's grace relationships were restored and, in some cases, deepened more than before. The point I failed to grasp was the need to continually invest in relationships with those we work alongside. When the fog rolls in relationships that are being invested in will help pave the way through. Growing relationships set the stage for meaningful discipleship and training. Stagnant relationships among leaders and the teams we lead bring little to no support and strength.

Every leader must develop other leaders or their leadership is severely limited in impact both in the immediate and future. We cannot lead through the chaos of our times without investing in other leaders. I have coached sports teams for many years and have learned teams that improve the most have individuals who are identified and mentored as leaders. You must develop and invest in players to lead before the games start for once the battles of competition begin you need leaders on the field to help navigate the team.

I believe this has been key to any coaching success I may have had. The reality is this takes time and if you are not fully convinced of the significance of building relationships you will move this down the list of priorities. To do so would be a big mistake. I speak from experience as one who had put more weight on my to-do list and less time with those closest to my leadership. God was gracious in reminding me over the years people are what matter and if I want to bear fruit in my home and the churches I serve, investing relationally is a non-negotiable.

A commitment to stay focused on foundational components

Keeping the main thing the main thing is difficult enough when the sailing is smooth it is exponentially more difficult when times are uncertain and chaotic. In the situation I have been sharing, due to the main concern being theological, specifically the gifts of the Holy Spirit and His role in a believer's life, we decided to focus on the foundational beliefs we shared as a church.

We renewed our call to bring the gospel to our community. The church name change resulted from this. This was the mission Jesus gave us and was the main thing we were supposed to be doing.

We also as elders led a foundations class walking through our statement of faith. When there are disagreements over issues that are not explicitly revealed in Scripture it is easy to lose sight of what is held in common. In our case, as a church, the issue was biblical truth. We wanted to regain unity around the main tenets of the Christian faith. Regaining clarity of what we believe and what we are supposed to be doing provided solid footing to move forward.

The challenging times are numerous and varied in the contexts we lead. As a family, it may be boundaries. It could be dealing with technology usage, rebellion, or clothing standards.

In your marriage, it could be growing debt, unexpected health issues, communication breakdown, or emotional breakdown. Any one or multiple issues can emerge and create times of confusion and uncertainty.

A business could have layoffs, benefit cuts, rearrangement of departments, and a host of other issues all of which bring uncertainty and a lack of clarity.

In each case getting back to the main thing for the reason each exists is essential. If not, the atmosphere will only become foggier and loss will come in one way or another.

Marriages during difficult times need to revisit the purpose God has for marriage relationships, namely oneness. This truth and picture of what our marriages are designed for, namely the spiritual, emotional, and physical intimacy that reflects Jesus' love for His Church, must once again be clarified. The "me" must become the "we" for the great "He".

As a leader in your marriage, you must be the one to take your spouse back to the purpose God brought you together. You cannot feed the conflict and chaos by directing attention and energy in multiple directions. You must not in pride refuse to admit your contributions to the conflict or to ask forgiveness. Do not wait for your spouse to step toward you. You take the first step and as many as are needed to lead your marriage back to the main purpose of why you are together in the first place.

When families are in disarray, they must be led back to why God brought them together. That is to unify around God's call to show His love and the parent's role to raise a generation of followers of Christ. It is not the school's job or anyone else's to raise or lead your children to live out your collective purpose. Repeat often with your children the reason God brought you together. When chaos reigns bring everyone together, restate the main thing, and orient direction and plan around that.

My battle with cancer has allowed my children to see it is not my battle alone. It is ours together. I need them with me. When I finished my radiation treatment a tradition the cancer centers have is to ring a bell at the last treatment. I rang the bell thankful for being done with all the treatments, but a far greater gratitude welled up within me as my children were with me. My children were able to see one aspect of our purpose as a family is to support and walk through the highs and lows of life together. I was able to talk about the need for and purpose of our family during this time.

Every team that faces confusing times needs to refocus on what is the main thing and that is becoming the best team they can. The egos and selfish agendas need to be tossed aside so the team can maximize its strength. The little "me" must be set aside so the big "we" can emerge.

Every department in the workplace must refocus on what their mission is. Personal conflicts and opinions must be set aside for the sake of the company's mission.

In every group, a leader(s) must step up and lead their people back to the main reason they are together. Lead those you love to keep the main thing the main thing. As I have heard said, "best change happens when you decide what should never change."

When leading through the doctrinal dissension after we took the step to spend time on teaching and focusing on the core beliefs, we all held in common, I then took time to teach a series that was the crux of the disagreement. We could not take that step until we had begun to build relationships and regain our focus on the main things. I say that to encourage you. Getting through those times will not happen overnight so don't rush through the steps you need to take. Allow the teaching, relationship building, and refocusing that is necessary to do their work.

Lead with other leaders together. Walk as an organization, family, or whatever context, together through the steps you must take. Then build on each firm step you take. I believe God is gracious in bringing greater growth as He did with us years ago. I am encouraged and instructed by the words of Tom Nelson,

"In times of great uncertainty and disruption, a common tendency is to get busier, work harder, and put in longer hours. As leaders, we tell ourselves if we simply do more and plan more, than things will work out better. It has been said that humans are the only species on the planet that when lost, simply go faster…. When you really don't know what to do, be honest with yourself. Be willing to say to others around you, "I don't know. When decisions are painfully difficult and choices limited, you can still love others well no matter what."[1]

Make consistent evaluation

To lead through the fog requires consistent evaluation on the front end. By that I mean evaluating yourself and your other leaders regularly. To lead through chaos and unpredictability requires making many strategic decisions. To have a deep influence in others' lives will require strategic decisions both for the leader and by the leader. These decisions must be intentional and directional. This requires leaders knowing the condition of their hearts and where they are leading others. It is necessary to wrestle with questions like: What is the goal I am leading my marriage toward? How am I going to train my children? How will I lead the department to greater personal growth and productivity? How will I help my team maximize our potential?

Those questions about leading others are much easier when we first ask questions to ourselves. Many leaders would benefit greatly from more self-evaluation. I believe the discipline of journaling has helped me over the years with regard to this. The Holy Spirit will not let me off the hook when I am consistently reading scripture and in prayer. The list below of questions may help you and your teams as you evaluate where you are at in regard to the condition of your heart and the direction of your energies. Perhaps walk through these now.

Have I decreased and Jesus increased during this past week? I wear a rubber band on my wrist that says in large print "He must Increase". What have your conversations been about? You more than Jesus? Who has gotten the praise for any successes? After all, this is the main thing!

What have I learned about God and living for Him that I didn't know last week? To quit learning is forfeiting the right to lead. Leaders learn. And only learners can lead.

Would my wife say she feels cherished? This requires you to know your wife well enough to know what makes her feel cherished. Not sure? Ask her.

Would I want my children to pray like I did this week? I know ouch!

Whom did I attempt to share the gospel with this week? If not, ask who I can share with today.

Who and how did I encourage someone to follow Jesus this week? Be specific in your evaluation.

Am I hiding anything that would displease God or hurt others? Secrets that revolve around issues of the heart can be deadly. Bring the dark temptations into the light of truth and accountable relationships. Be quick to confess and repent.

If I were to stop my leadership role today would the work continue without me? Focus on investing in others and especially other leaders. We cannot have a deepening influence if we are not equipping others.

What would my wife, children, and teams say were my priorities this week?

It is not hard to see where personal evaluation can reorient our lives toward what we have been called to do. Personal evaluation is a must to regain direction and deepen influence as leaders.

Evaluating ourselves well on the front end bears great fruit when we seek to lead others through difficult times. Dictators make decisions based on personal preferences or selfish gratification. But leading those you love means we make decisions based on what is best for those we are leading. Decision-making out of love and decision-making out of control or power look very different. When we keep a pulse of grace in our hearts the pull toward self and control lessens. When control lessens surrender to what God has called us to do increases.

CHAPTER EIGHT

Leading to the End – The Endurance of a Leader

I read a study a few years ago on historical and contemporary leaders. This study reached some conclusions and one which grabbed my attention was that few leaders finish their life well. In track terms, they faded on the final lap. Their focus, enthusiasm, and passion which sustained them over the years had been left to wither and wane as the years passed. It wasn't just them that paid a price so too did those they led and sought to lead. How tragic. Helping, guiding, and loving others toward growth got set aside in a later season of life. The season that can have potentially the greatest impact revealed the leaders studied lost sight of the goal. Of the privilege. Of the opportunity.

I want to finish well. I am at the age where my energy is not near where it was, and my focus gets lost easier. My one-time sharp memory is now unable to retain tasks and facts like before. I never needed reminders for years now each day my phone chimes to remind me of even the most basic things. Just yesterday I went to the garage and when I got there, I had to take time to mentally drum up why I was there. Worse yet after going out for pizza I put leftovers in a to-go box and when leaving put the box on top of the van to talk with my son. You know what is coming. I got in the car and several miles down the road it hit me. We stopped on the side of the road hoping by some miracle the pizza was still on top, unfortunately it was gone. I instead was left with another reminder life isn't getting easier. In the midst of all I have talked about in this book of how to have a lasting influence marked by grace begs the question how do we sustain our commitment to the end of this life?

- **Endure with Focus**

I can relate now to those who have led for years tired, physically compromised, and often feeling out of touch with younger generations. While those are realities they are not excuses. God calls us to run the race He has set before us and part of running that race is to finish well. The author of the New Testament book of Hebrews calls Christians to *"lay aside very weight, and sin which clings so closely, and let us run with endurance the race that is set before us, looking to Jesus the author and perfecter of our faith, who for the joy set before Him endured the cross, despising the shame, and is seated at the right hand of God."* Hebrews 12:1b-2 (ESV)

What is most striking from this passage is the focus needed that make endurance possible. The words "looking to Jesus" are especially instructive for us all. We do not look at our feet or others' feet in the race but focus on our Savior and the example He set.

The example of Jesus was He finished the race that led Him to the cross. Even when near the end of His life on earth He faced great resistance, attempts on His life, rejection, mockery, and even abandonment by friends. He didn't quit. He wasn't sidetracked or defeated by all that surrounded Him. He stands as our perfect example of how to endure.

It is this type of focus you and I will need to finish strong. Health setbacks, relational strain, loss, disappointment, and discouragement will surround us all. The question is not will we experience those, the question is whether will we persevere through them. Grit is needed. A roll-up-your-sleeves and push-on mindset is required to keep growing, maturing, and investing in others' lives.

This is and has been the season I am in right now. Cancer scares and surgeries, increasing fatigue, loss of my parents, and children struggling all tempt me to mentally check out and disengage from people and pursuits. I know however, that is not God's will nor my heart's desire. So, I resolve to push myself and by faith remain engaged in serving and loving people well. I know to be able to do that adjustments are necessary. I must be realistic and accept my limits. I have had to humbly admit the load I once could carry is no longer healthy or even realistic.

I have shared I was privileged to pastor a wonderful church family in Cokato, Minnesota. We as a church grew together through good and tough times and experienced the move of God in many ways. With several staff to mentor, a large elder board and growing counseling and administrative tasks the load or responsibilities I needed to carry became heavier. When the cancer and multiple metastasis came, so did the heavy fatigue and diminishing strength. Even though I had all the support a pastor could need I had to honestly admit I could not serve the church the way they needed. I grieved as the spiritual and numerical growth is what I had prayed for was taking place and I would not be there to continue to watch it. Every pastor and leader dreams of what we were experiencing. Great unity allowed us to make tough staff adjustments, become missional throughout our ministries, and build several million-dollar new facilities. Amazing growth in unity, converts and discipleship was taking place.

God confirmed His leading for me to return to the smaller church in Stanley. Both church elder boards confirmed this as we all prayed. I celebrate the work of God in and through Highland Community Church in Cokato as it continues to grow under newer and younger leadership. I celebrate what God is doing in the church I now pastor in Stanley, Wisconsin. God has graciously allowed me to serve in a way in which there is a purposeful pacing. Purposeful pacing is not as much to conserve strength but to maximize daily impact. It is of very little value to pace myself and live a little longer if I am not seeking to impact lives for God. So, I run with purpose and the pacing helps me maximize my days.

To endure in leadership, you will need to run in such a way that you can finish well. You must run with a dogged determination to keep growing. Too many leaders are knocked down by the storms. Too many lay on the side of the road broken by this fallen world. Whether they experience the fruitfulness of impacting lives with longevity is determined by their commitment to growing in maturity. Strategic leadership is not maturing leadership. Positional leadership is not fruit-producing leadership. Faithful leadership is where the fruit is. Faithfulness in leading in our marriages, homes, and with our teams is where deep influence occurs. When are committed to growing in maturity, we are able to see an increasing harvest of the fruit of impact. It becomes a balance of loving, growing, and serving hard yet pacing ourselves by refining the direction of where we invest ourselves. It's more than simply enduring, its endurance which is married to growth that produces lasting fruit.

You may, like I had to, step away from a situation or location to finish well. In the seasons of life, and especially the later seasons of life, lies a great temptation to gauge our future plans according to financial or selfish gain. We are told to wait until we get to the retirement age than we can really live. When it comes to living in an overflow of grace to influence others there is no such thing as retirement. I would exhort you instead to evaluate how will you impact others for Christ in the next season of your life. How can you best do that? In what context can you have the greatest impact? What pace is needed to maximize your day?

No one can lead well operating at warp speed. No matter how young you are, if you want to endure the surrounding challenges and finish well learn to pace yourself in a way you thrive and keep your spiritual, emotional, and relational tanks full. To keep your tanks full is to engage where divine refills are most likely to occur. Time with God in reading and prayer, and time with other Christians are all places God uses to strengthen us. Quality and quantity time with your spouse and children. Exercise. Time with friends who energize you. These must be priorities on our calendars.

Every leader has limits and we are prideful to think otherwise. We have limited gifts. Limited time. Limited energy and limited maturity and experience. Paul Tripp accurately speaks to this,

"You are not a package of strengths, gifts, and experiences; you are also a collection of weaknesses and susceptibilities. It is here the gospel is a sweet encouragement. We do not have to fear our limits because God doesn't send us out on our own; where He sends us, He goes to. We do not have to curse our weaknesses because our weaknesses are a workroom for His grace."[1]

The older we get the limits increase. Yet even then God is at work. If we are to lead those we love until Jesus takes us home, we need to be mindful of our limits so we can maximize the time and energy we do have. So too we can leverage the growth God has and is bringing into our lives. God is not done with you. Don't let anyone tell you any different.

The limits are not to stifle us, but I believe it is crucial to lock in on what matters most. Until we reach the other side we live, relate, and lead with limits. Don't fight them for what God calls us to do we will be able to accomplish in His strength. You can look at the limits and become depressed or you can pour your energy into those closest to you. You're going to have to push yourself at times to leave the confines of your recliner and go out and talk with people. Use your time and energy to bring encouragement to all those you have invested in over the years by praying, calling, or writing.

All these efforts will help you keep your tanks full and provide you with a rhythm of living conducive to endurance.

Long-term effective leadership in any capacity takes courage. You and I will face opposition. You will endure accusations, misunderstandings, and questions. At times you will face relationship strains. You will feel inadequate, weak, and overwhelmed. You will feel undervalued. You can't throw in the towel. God's grace, presence, and power are more than enough to allow you to press on.

I remember visiting Dad one time in the nursing home, and I asked him like I always did, "how are you, Dad?" He surprised me with the reply, "I feel useless son". I teared up and said something along the lines of, "Dad I need to know how to finish my life well. I need you to show me. Please don't say you're useless". What I was trying to say to Dad, and to you who read this, the way you endure especially in the later seasons of life is the exclamation point of deep influence. All the ways we poured into others and sought to live out of the overflow of a heart of grace find added impact when we persevere through obstacles, health, and old age. Our children, grandchildren, and the younger men and women we have invested in must see what it looks like to finish well. Leading those you love well means you finish well.

There are many examples in the Bible of men and women who finished life well. I encourage you to read about Moses, Joshua, Elijah, David, and others. Great examples of loving, living, growing, and serving until their final breath. Learn from Solomon and many other kings who got sucked into the lie more is better, whose character eroded and did not finish well.

I learn much about a proper focus in living from the Apostle Paul. He says in Philippians 1:21, *"To live is Christ to die is gain."* (NIV) For Paul, it was all about Christ. Even if God should allow him to go through trials, he lived with a laser-like focus, as evidenced by 2 Corinthians 4:16-18:

Therefore, we do not lose heart. Though outwardly we are wasting away, yet inwardly we are being renewed day by day. For our light and momentary troubles are achieving an eternal glory that far outweighs them all. So we fix our eyes not on what is seen, but on what is unseen, since what is seen is temporary, but what is unseen is eternal. (NIV)

In Acts 13 we read about Paul and Barnabas as they travel to various locations sharing the good news of Jesus. One day while in the synagogue, we'd call a church, they spoke. In the midst of their address, this statement was made, *"For David after He had served the purpose of God in his generation, fell asleep..."* (Acts 13:36 ESV)

I find these verses compelling and challenging. What a statement to have made about you after you died, "he served the purposes of God in his generation". Paul and David serve to you and me, as examples of how to finish well. Like these two men, we will experience times when we sin, stumble, and blow it. Times we regret deeply. Yet none of those things cancel the call of God to finish well.

When I go to bed at night, I often ask myself a question. I ask, "did I love well today? Did I love God and others?" If I can answer in the affirmative, it was a day well lived in my opinion. Even more, I believe it was a well-lived day in God's eyes. The more days I string together of loving and following Jesus well my influence deepens. I get goose-bumps with the awareness I can speak ahead into generations out of a heart that loves and grows today. That is fuel for my soul. That is motivation to get out of bed when weakness weighs on me like a wet blanket. I know God wants me to love and speak to others; to have a deep influence so I can walk into that with the assurance that I "can do all things through Christ who strengthens me" (Philippians 4:13 NIV). So too can you. Stay focused on growing spiritually and relationally throughout your life. Don't quit.

Like David, might it be said of you and I at the time God takes us home from this earth "we served the purpose of God" in our generation.

- **Endure in community**

No leader can finish well by personal resolve alone. We need a vibrant, loving, faithful community. Spiritual friends. Brothers and sisters in Christ who make the presence of God visible through comfort and encouragement. God has blessed me beyond measure with close believing friends who whether geographically close or at a distance bring strength. I feel responsible to support them and help them serve faithfully and I know they feel the same.

My heart gets stirred when I hear about and see people laughing, crying, and praying together. Friends relying upon Christ together. Here is the key (for young and old alike). If the ultimate purpose of our journey is Jesus and living for His glory and to finish well, your close friends need to be those who share and encourage you in that purpose. We probably all have several friends, but our close friends must be anchored in their commitment to living for Christ. If they are not, you will be sidetracked and begin to live for yourself. That is the orientation of the lost world.

There is a man in the Bible who had everything. Surrounded by a household of people and riches and wealth, he lacked nothing. His portfolio was like no other and his renown was like no other. He wrote a journal about what he observed and concluded in life. The man is Solomon, and the journal is the book in the Bible, Ecclesiastes.

Solomon, the son of King David, inherited the throne and was blessed with great wisdom and wealth. This is the author of the Book of Ecclesiastes. In his journal we read this: *"There was a man all alone; he had neither son nor brother. There was no end to his toil, yet his eyes were not content with his wealth. "For whom am I toiling," he asked, "and why am I depriving myself of enjoyment?" This too is meaningless—a miserable business! Two are better than one, because they have a good return for their labor: If either of them falls down, one can help the other up. But pity anyone who falls and has no one to help them up. Also, if two lie down together, they will keep warm. But how can one keep warm alone? Though one may be overpowered, two can defend themselves. A cord of three strands is not quickly broken." Ecclesiastes 4:8-12(NIV)*

Solomon was in a sea of people but had no close friends. He even wondered why he was depriving himself of the enjoyment of friends. Not coincidently he failed to serve God in his final years. He needed the strength, accountability, and encouragement of a spiritual friend. Take it from one who knew, two are better than one. Sadly, he learned it too late.

When reading through the New Testament epistles you can't miss the many people who walked with the apostle Paul. He lists numerous persons who helped him endure. Who are those walking with you and encouraging you toward growth and fruitfulness? If you have no one ask yourself, who do I see who can walk with me in this way? God did not design us to walk alone. We grow best in the spiritual community, and we will finish best in the spiritual community.

My closest friend John and I meet on Wednesday mornings for breakfast. We order French toast 95 percent of the time. We share, laugh, and pray together. Every Wednesday morning, I am reminded I am not running the race alone. And that I am committed to helping John finish well and he is to me. I can think of many mornings we shared how good it was to meet and the encouragement we received even though we really didn't discuss much. I call it the ministry of presence. Our prayers reveal a desire to impact those we love from hearts moved by the grace of God. Just being together and allowing the Spirit of God to bring us strength through His presence with us is helping me endure.

Find travel buddies who like you are striving for eternal impact. Spiritual friends who can support each other so as to finish well.

Conclusion

My dad suffered the last three years of his life from dementia and each time I left visiting him I grieved as another part of my dad seemed to die. I stood by his bedside many times, but this last one was hardest as my dad had just passed away. As I wept, I tried to process what this meant. For him, I believe he was with His Savior Jesus, that is what really mattered. For me, my model, hero, and friend was gone. Dad was far from perfect but his love for Mom and us as siblings and so many others called out to me to do the same. My leader was gone, and I felt an immediate void. I am not sure about my siblings, but I felt a mantle passed on to provide leadership for Mom and among my siblings. To this day I have tried to carry that mantle. That focus was sharpened the day Dad passed and has traveled with me. It is like I can hear him say "Lead well son".

One day I will be leaving this earth, and I wonder what Cyndy and those I invested my life in will say. I know they all will be able to say I made mistakes. That is for sure. But will they be able to say I was an example of love and a model of servant leadership? Even more, will they say my life was about loving, exalting, and pointing people to Jesus Christ? Will they think of God's grace changing me through my days?

This book has not been about strategic or positional leadership but about the deep influence possible by leaders. That is leadership that connects at the heart level.

I have endeavored in these pages to share my heart and what I believe with all my being is the call on my life. I have prayed I could also pass on to you the reader encouragement and direction for you to have a deep influence on the people God has brought and will bring into your life.

I want to remind you as you make the shift toward making a deep impact from a heart filled with grace you do not do so alone. In Christ, the presence, glory, and grace of God is with you and for you. His glorious grace will meet every need and empower your efforts toward deep influence.

Now may God continue to pour into your heart greater and greater grace so as to splash over into the lives of those you lead.

Appendix

STEPS TO PEACE WITH GOD through a relationship with CHRIST

1. **God's Plan**—Peace and Life. God loves you and wants you to experience His peace and life. The Bible says: "For God so loved the world that He gave His only begotten Son, that whoever believes in Him should not perish but have everlasting life" (John 3:16).
2. **Our Problem**—Separation. Being at peace with God is not automatic, because by nature you are separated from God. The BIBLE says: "For all have sinned and fall short of the glory of God" (Romans 3:23).
3. **God's Remedy**—The Cross. God's love bridges the gap of separation between God and you. When Jesus Christ died on the cross and rose from the grave, He paid the penalty for your sins. The BIBLE says: "He personally carried the load of our sins in his own body when he died on the cross" (1 Peter 2:24, tlb).
4. **Our Response**—Receive Christ. You cross the bridge into God's family when you receive Christ by personal invitation. The BIBLE says: "But as many as received Him, to them He gave the right to become children of God, even to those who believe in His name" (John 1:12).

To receive Christ you need to do four things:

1. ADMIT your spiritual need. "I am a sinner."
2. REPENT and be willing to turn from your sin.
3. BELIEVE that Jesus Christ died for you on the cross.
4. RECEIVE, through prayer, Jesus Christ into your heart and life. Christ says, "Behold, I stand at the door and knock. If anyone hears My voice and opens the door, I will come in" (Revelation 3:20). Claim the promise, "Whoever calls upon the name of the Lord will be saved" (Romans 10:13).

Let this prayer guide you: Dear Lord Jesus, I know that I am a sinner and need Your forgiveness. I believe that You died for my sins. I chose now to turn from my sins. I now invite You to come into my heart and life. I want to trust and follow You as Lord and Savior. In Jesus' name, Amen.

Billygraham.org

Endnotes

Chapter One – The Call to Lead
[1] Matthew Miklasz, *A Normal Guy, 2018.* Halo Publishing International 1100 NW Loop San Antonio, Texas 78213.
[2] Copyright 1984-2002. Target Training Center, Ltd.
[3] John Maxwell, The Five Levels of Leadership, 2011, New York, NY 10017
[4] Loder, Ted. *Guerillas of Grace.* Innisfree Press. 1984.

Chapter Two – Leading Yourself
[1] Tim Clinton 1st Faith Words – Turn *your Life Around* ed. Hatchette Book Group USA 1271 Avenue of the Americas New York, NY. 10020
[2] Wolgemuth, Robert. *The Most Important Place on Earth.* Thomas Nelson, 2004. Page 93,95.

Chapter Three – Leading Your Spouse
[1] Max Lucado In the Grip of Grace 1996 Word Publishing, Dallas Texas 75039

Chapter Four – Leading Your Children
[1] Results taken from research conducted by the National Fatherhood Initiative and can be found at http://fatherhood.org/media/consequences
[2] Diann Ackard et al, American Journal of Preventative Medicine 1(January 30, 2006) 59-66
[3] Planet, Paul. "Hugging Is an Excellent Source of Free Dopamine." The Dopamine Project Newsletter. July 11, 2011.
[4] Rick Johnson – *Better Dads, Stronger Dads* Revell Books, (May 1, 2006)

Chapter Five – Leading Your Teams
[1] 2008 The Coaching Center In cooperation with the Colombia Partnership & On Purpose Ministry
[2] Dan Reiland, Confident leader Become One Stay One, 2020 Thomas Nelson Books Nashville, Tennessee

Chapter Six – Leading Through Trials

Chapter seven – Leading Through the fog

[1] Tom Nelson, *The Flourishing Pastor 2021 page 205,* Intervarsity Press PO Box 1400, Downers Grove, Il. 60515-1426

Chapter Eight – Leading to the End

[1] Lead 2020 by Paul David Tripp Published by Crossway. 1300 Crescent Street Wheaton, Illinois 60187